Early MiG Fighters

in Action

By Hans-Heiri Stapfer

Color by Don Greer

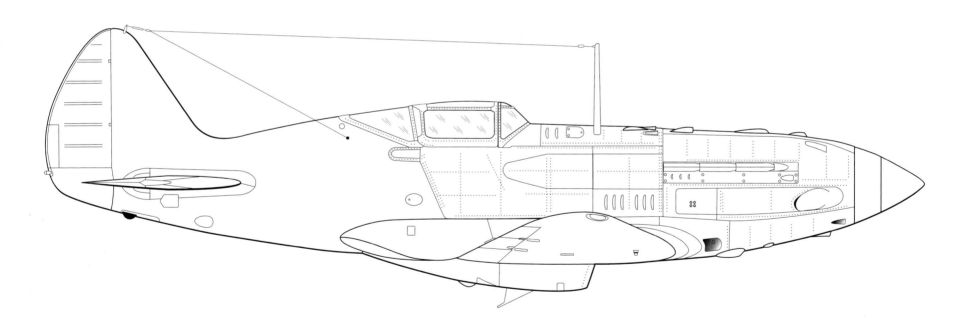

Squadron Signal
Publications

Aircraft Number 204

MW00613243

Cover: Lieutenant Aleksey N. Katrisht, Squadron Leader in the 20. IAP (20th *Istrebitel'niy Aviapolk* — 20th Fighter Aviation Regiment) of the PVO (*Protivovozdushnogo Oborona* — Anti-Air Defense Forces) downs a Dornier Do 217 on the night of 21-22 September 1941 by ramming it after exhausting his ammunition supply. Katrisht was able to land his MiG-3 with minor damage, and for this action became a Hero of the Soviet Union on 28 October 1941. During the Great Patriotic War, Katrisht shot down an additional fourteen enemy aircraft. In the early 1980s, he became a Colonel-General and Deputy Supreme Commander of the Warsaw Pact Air Forces in Europe. (Painting by Don Greer)

If you have any photographs of aircraft, armor, soldiers or ships of any nation, particularly wartime snapshots, why not share them with us and help make Squadron/Signal's books all the more interesting and complete in the future? Any photograph sent to us will be copied and the original returned. The donor will be fully credited for any photos used. Please send them to:

Squadron/Signal Publications, Inc.
1115 Crowley Drive
Carrollton, TX 75006

Если у вас есть фотографии самолётов, вооружения, солдат или кораблей любой страны, особенно, снимки времён войны, поделитесь с нами и помогите сделать новые книги издательства Эскадрон/Сигнал ещё интереснее. Мы переснимем ваши фотографии и вернём оригиналы. Имена приславших снимки будут сопровождать все опубликованные фотографии. Пожалуйста, присылайте фотографии по адресу:

Squadron/Signal Publications, Inc.
1115 Crowley Drive
Carrollton, TX 75006

軍用機、装甲車両、兵士、軍艦などの写真を所持しておられる方はいらっしゃいませんか？どの国のものでも結構です。作戦中に撮影されたものが特に良いのです。Squadron/Signal社の出版する刊行物において、このような写真は内容を一層充実し、興味深くすることができます。当方にお送り頂いた写真は、複写の後お返しいたします。出版物中に写真を使用した場合は、必ず提供者のお名前を明記させて頂きます。お写真は下記にご送付ください。

Squadron/Signal Publications, Inc.
1115 Crowley Drive
Carrollton, TX 75006

Acknowledgements and Photo Credits

Jozef And'al
Dan Antoniu
Heinz Birkholz
Robert Bock
Bundesarchiv Koblenz
Nigel A. Eastaway
ECPA France
Robert Gretzyngier
Jet & Prop Magazine
Volker Koos

Sergei Kuznetsov
Hans-Joachim Mau
Andrzej Morgala
Klaus Niska
G. F. Petrov
George Punka
RART
Wolfgang Tamme
Mariusz Zimny

▸ Three extraordinarily colorful MiG-3s at a handover ceremony at Moscow-Khodinka airfield on 23 February 1942. These fighters were destined for the 172. *IAP* and were the last MiG-3s built. They were assembled from components left behind at Khodinka when State Aircraft Factory 1 was evacuated to Kuybishev (now Samara). The third MiG-3 carries an RSI-4 '*Malyutka*' radio, as the starboard-mounted antenna mast indicates. Each of the three MiG-3s is equipped with a total of six RO-82 rails to accommodate the RS-82 unguided missile. The MiGs were painted white overall with 'All' Blue undersurfaces. All markings were red. The inscriptions on the three MiG-3 read (front to back) "*Za Rodinu*" ("For the Motherland"), "*Za Stalina*" ("For Stalin"), and "*Za Partii Bolshevikov*" ("For the Party of the Bolsheviks"). (G.F. Petrov)

Introduction

The most prominent manufacturer of fighter aircraft in the former Soviet Union is arguably the MiG (for **Mi**koyan + **G**urevich) Design Bureau. The star of Artyom I. Mikoyan and Mikhail I. Gurevich began to rise during the Korean War, when the swept-wing MiG-15 (NATO code name 'Fagot') was a very unwelcome surprise to United Nations pilots fighting over the Korean peninsula. From then until the demise of the Soviet Union in 1991, the MiG Design Bureau had a near monopoly on the supply of tactical fighters to the *VVS* (*Voenno-Vozdushne Sili* — Soviet Army Air Forces) and countries in Moscow's sphere of influence.

While post-World War II MiG fighters such as the MiG-15, MiG-21 'Fishbed,' and MiG-25 'Foxbat' have featured prominently in the headlines of the world press, it is not generally known that the MiG Design Bureau built a number of formidable fighters during the "Great Patriotic War" (as World War II was known in the Soviet Union). However, these superb fighters were not allowed to develop beyond the prototype stage in order not to interrupt the production lines of Yakovlev and Lavochkin.

On 8 December 1939 an OPO (*Opytnyi Otdel* — Experimental Design Department) was established, with Artyom I. Mikoyan as its head. Artyom Ivanovich Mikoyan (1905-1970) was the younger brother of Anastasy I. Mikoyan, the Commissar for Commerce, who had studied American foods and introduced, in addition to other products, a whole range of ice creams to the Soviet Union.

Sons of a carpenter, the Mikoyan brothers grew up in Armenia. Artyom graduated from the high school at Tblisi, Georgia, and became a mechanic before he was drafted into the Red Army. During 1931, he entered the *VVA* (*Voenno-vozdushnaya Akademiya* — Air Force Academy). He subsequently became a Chief Designer in the Polikarpov Design Bureau.

When Artyom's OPO was formed in the facilities of the State Aircraft Factory at Khodinka, one-third of Polikarpov's engineers decided to join the new department. On 15 March 1940, the Mikoyan Experimental Design Department received the status of an *OKB* (*Opytno Konstruktorskoe Byuro* — Experimental Design Bureau).

Mikoyan's deputy was Mikhail Iosifovich Gurevich (1892-1976), who was born near Kursk in the Ukraine. He studied advanced mathematics at Kharkov (now Ukraine), but after expulsion for his revolutionary activities, he went to France in 1913 and studied at the University of Montpellier. For a while Gurevich was assigned to the Douglas Company at Santa Monica, California, to assist the Soviet license production of the Douglas DC-3. In late 1938, he joined the Polikarpov OKB.

I-200

During 1939, the Polikarpov *OKB* began the design of a high altitude interceptor, Project 'Kh.' When the Experimental Design Department under Artyom I. Mikoyan was formed, the Project Kh research data was transferred to the new *OPO*.

Several defects and teething problems delayed development, and the young Experimental Design Department was forced to accommodate the only supercharged engine available at that time, the Mikulin AM-35A, with an output of 1,400 hp above 5,000 meters (16,404 feet). The AM-35A had been designed for the heavy TB-7 heavy bomber and lacked provision for a cannon firing through the propeller hub, in sharp contrast to the Klimov M-105 engine that powered the contemporary LaGG-3 and Yak-1 fighters. Armament of two ShKAS 7.62 mm (.30-caliber) machine guns and a single Berezin UBS 12.7 mm (.50-caliber) machine gun was selected for the fighter but was not installed in the first two I-200 prototypes.

▼ The first I-200 prototype (serial number 01) made its maiden flight on 5 April 1940 and during trials attained a speed of 648 km/h (403 mph), some 50 km/h (31 mph) faster than the contemporary Messerschmitt Bf 109E-3 then undergoing testing in Germany. (G.F. Petrov)

▼ The second I-200 (serial number 02) was equipped with an exhaust outlet shutter at the rear of the oil cooler fairing. Two slots for cooling were added in front of the canopy. (Robert Bock)

The AM-35A engine drove a VISh-22Ye propeller. For the intended high-altitude missions, the pilot was provided with a KPA-3bis oxygen system. To the greatest extent possible, the new fighter was built from pine and birch plywood as well as fabric, materials that were available in nearly unlimited quantities in the Soviet Union.

The first I-200 (serial number 01) left the assembly shop on 30 March 1940 and made its maiden flight 5 April 1940. The I-200 was introduced to the public on 1 May 1940 over Red Square during the May Day parade at Moscow. The second prototype of the I-200 (serial number 02) first flew on 9 May 1940. The main differences between the two prototypes were in the provisions for cooling the engine and engine oil.

The I-200's handling qualities left much to be desired. Its longitudinal stability was very poor, its flight controls were heavy in all three axes, and its landing speed was very high. It became clear that an average pilot could not master the fighter. Improvements had to be made, and the MiG Design Bureau worked under great pressure to rectify all shortcomings. However, in the hands of an experienced pilot, the I-200 unveiled its potential during high-speed factory test trials on 22 May 1940, when test pilot Arkadi N. Yekatov reached 648 km/h (403 mph) in I-200 Number 1, and Major Stepan P. Suprun achieved a speed of 651 km/h (405 mph) at an altitude of 7,000 meters (22,966 feet) in I-200 Number 2. These speeds were over 50 km/h (31 mph) faster than the contemporary Messerschmitt Bf 109E-3, the standard Luftwaffe fighter at that time. With the I-200, the Soviet Union now had in its inventory not only one of the world's fastest fighters but also one of the most dangerous to fly.

The first and second prototypes of the I-200 were subsequently handed over for State Acceptance Trials at Chalovskaya Air Base on 29 August 1940. These tests lasted until 12 September 1940. (▶ 7)

I-200 Prototypes

I-200 Number 1

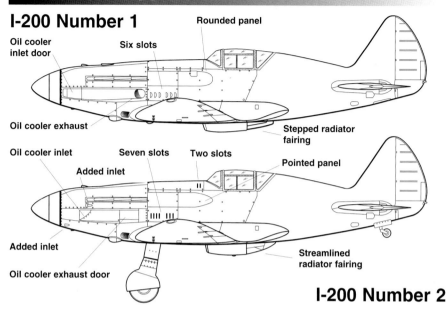

Rounded panel
Oil cooler inlet door
Six slots
Oil cooler exhaust
Stepped radiator fairing

Oil cooler inlet
Seven slots
Two slots
Added inlet
Pointed panel
Added inlet
Oil cooler exhaust door
Streamlined radiator fairing

I-200 Number 2

▼ The second prototype of the I-200 during State Acceptance trials. I-200 Number 2 first flew on 9 May 1940. No markings were ever applied to its overall silver finish. Neither of the I-200 prototypes was armed. (Sergei Kuznetsov)

▼ The modified I-200 Number 2 during spin tests with the Scientific Research Institute of the Soviet Air Force at Chalovskaya. The canopy has been removed, and the oil cooler and its fairing on the engine cowling have been deleted. (G.F. Petrov)

Development

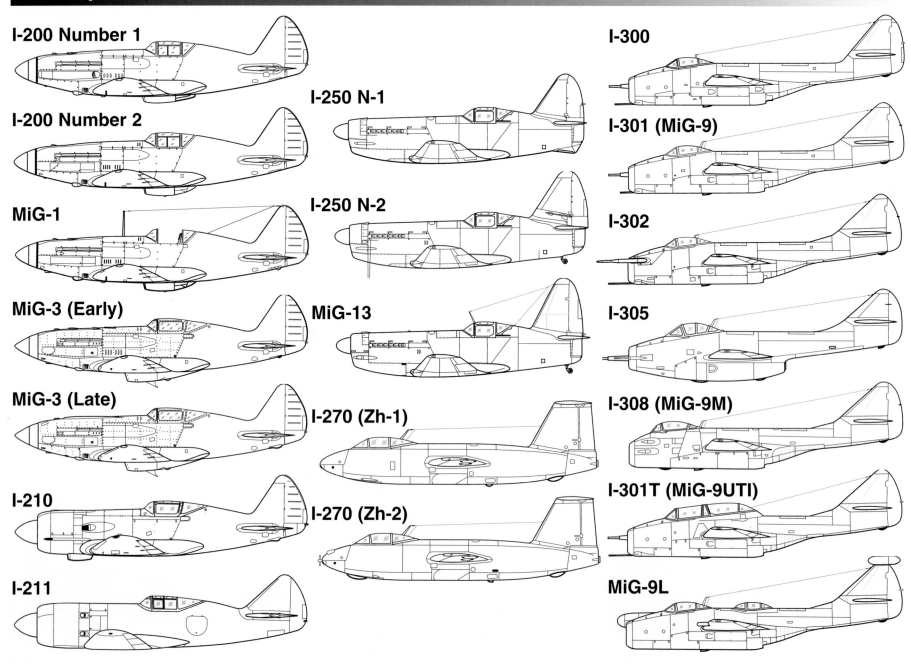

I-200 Number 1

I-200 Number 2

MiG-1

MiG-3 (Early)

MiG-3 (Late)

I-210

I-211

I-250 N-1

I-250 N-2

MiG-13

I-270 (Zh-1)

I-270 (Zh-2)

I-300

I-301 (MiG-9)

I-302

I-305

I-308 (MiG-9M)

I-301T (MiG-9UTI)

MiG-9L

MiG-1

The third production I-200 (serial number 03) became the pattern aircraft for initial mass production of the aircraft. GAZ-1 (*Gosudarstvenny Aviatsionny Zavod 1* — State Aircraft Factory 1) at Moscow-Khodinka was selected for this task. GAZ-1, Russia's first aircraft factory, was the former DUX factory of pre-revolution days and had built Farman, Sopwith, and Nieuport fighters under license.

I-200 Number 3 became the first MiG fighter to be armed. The plane received a single Berezin UBS 12.7 mm (.50-caliber) machine gun mounted on the aircraft centerline and two ShKAS 7.62 mm (.30-caliber) machine guns, one placed on either side of the Berezin UBS. All three machine guns were mounted above the Mikulin AM-35A engine with blast tubes over their muzzles. Technical problems with the S2K-26 armament synchronization gear delayed the maiden flight, which eventually took place on 6 June 1940.

The third prototype I-200 differed in a number of details from the second. The canopy, which opened to the starboard side on the first two I-200s and was not jettisonable in case of an emergency, was deleted from the third prototype. Engine cooling air scoops and oil cooler air inlets were revised yet again.

Like the first two prototypes, the third initially lacked a radio, but during the course of the factory test trials, an RSI-3 'Orel' (RSI: *Radiostanciya dlya Istrebitelei* — radio for fighter) was installed on the third prototype in a compartment just behind the cockpit. The radio required an antenna mast, which was mounted to starboard in front of the canopy. An antenna cable ran from the leading edge of the tail to the antenna mast, and a lead-in entered the radio compartment on the starboard side of the fuselage just behind the cockpit.

The first two I-200 prototypes had a square-shaped upper main wheel door, but this door on the third I-200 was smaller and trapezoid-shaped, and the main landing gear door had a rectangular access panel. The first two prototypes had flush tailwheel doors, but the tailwheel doors of the number three prototype were bulged.

The third prototype was equipped to accommodate two RO-82 rails under the wing in order to launch RS-82 unguided rockets. It was also equipped with an FS-155 landing light in the port wing leading edge, unlike the first two prototypes. All subsequent MiG-3s were equipped with a FS-155 landing light in the port wing as well.

I-200 Number 3 was assigned to the *Lyotno Issledovatel'ski Institut* (Flight Research Institute) for State Acceptance Trials beginning 12 August 1940. With a top speed of 628 km/h (390 mph), the I-200 was considerably faster than the Luftwaffe's standard fighter, the Bf 109E-3, but it was far from being a pilot's airplane like the German Messerschmitt. It had poor longitudinal stability, heavy controls, and a tendency to stall at the slightest provocation. Spin recovery was nearly impossible. In addition, maintenance and rearming of the I-200 was much more difficult and time-consuming than on the Bf 109E-3. Nevertheless, on May 25, 1940 the I-200 was formally ordered into production by the *NKAP* (*Narodny Komissariat Aviatsionnoi Promyshlennosti* — People's Commissariat for the Aircraft Industry).

The I-200 had already come to be known unofficially within the MiG Design Bureau as the 'MiG-1' when in early December 1940 the All-Union Communist Party decided that the military designations of fighter aircraft should be replaced by a prefix based on the name of the Design Bureau where the plane had been designed. By written order of the *VVS* on January 6, 1941, the acronym 'MiG' was officially assigned to the new fighter.

I-200 Number 3 was the only 'MiG-1' to be built. It served as a pattern aircraft for the mass production of the new fighter at GAZ-1, which began with MiG-3 serial number 04. (▶ 8)

▲ The third prototype I-200 (serial number 03) became the first I-200 to be armed. It was equipped with a Berezin UBS 12.7 mm (.50-caliber) machine gun and two ShKAS 7.62 mm (.30-caliber) machine guns placed above the engine. The canopy was deleted. This was the only 'MiG-1' to be built, and it served as a pattern for mass production at GAZ-1. (G.F. Petrov)

MiG-1 Development

I-200 Number 2

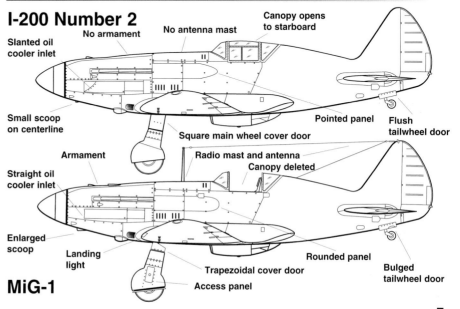

Slanted oil cooler inlet — No armament — No antenna mast — Canopy opens to starboard

Small scoop on centerline — Square main wheel cover door — Pointed panel — Flush tailwheel door

Armament — Radio mast and antenna — Canopy deleted

Straight oil cooler inlet

Enlarged scoop — Landing light — Trapezoidal cover door — Access panel — Rounded panel — Bulged tailwheel door

MiG-1

MiG-3

The MiG-1 had several shortcomings, which were detected during the factory tests and the State Acceptance Trials, and a new version incorporating several improvements was quickly developed. There was an intensive research program carried out by the MiG Design Bureau, and full-scale models were tested in the huge T-101 and T-104 wind tunnels of the *TsAGI* (*Tsentral'niy Aero-Gidrodinamicheskiy Institut* — Central Aero-Hydrodynamics Institute) at Kratovo.

German design solutions influenced the development and detail improvement of the MiG-3 through its production cycle. A total of five brand-new Regensburg-built Bf 109E-3s had been purchased from the Messerschmitt factory in May 1940 by the Soviet Union. The fighters were delivered in crates by train and assembled by Messerschmitt employees in a hangar at Khodinka, the Central Airport of Moscow. Tests of the Bf 109E-3 were conducted at the *NIIVVS* (*Nauchno Ispitatel'niy Institut Voyenno-Vozdushikh Sil* — Scientific Research Institute of the Soviet Air Force) at Chalovskaya Air Base. The design and construction of the Bf 109E-3 had a major influence on contemporary Soviet fighter designs, including the new MiG fighter.

The new MiG-3 differed in a number of details from the MiG-1. The most notable difference was the enlarged rear glazing provided to the MiG-3. The cockpit canopy, which had been eliminated from the MiG-1, was reintroduced on the MiG-3. The canopy of the MiG-3 was aft-sliding, in contrast to that of the two first I-200 prototypes, which had opened to starboard.

The oil cooler inlets on both sides of the engine cowling were redesigned on the MiG-3, and the small inlet mounted below the first engine exhaust stack was moved back to its original location as installed on the second I-200. Production MiG-3s had six ventilation slots on either side of the fuselage immediately aft of the oil cooler exhaust shutter, unlike the MiG-1, which had seven such slots.

On the MiG-3 a undercarriage position indicator was placed on the wing upper surfaces, a feature lacking on the MiG-1 and one which was copied from the Messerschmitt Bf 109E-3. The hinged wheel cover flaps, which were attached to the main wheel doors of the I-200 prototypes, were deleted and replaced by a cover door installed on the fuselage at the inner edge of each main wheel well. Two small rectangular doors on the MiG-3 replaced the upper trapezoid-shaped main wheel door of the MiG-1. On the main wheel cover door, a stiffening gusset was added, replacing the rectangular access hatch found on the main wheel door of the three I-200s. The I-200s had flush main wheel doors, while all MiG-3s had a triangle-shaped bulge on their lower main wheel doors. The MiG-3 was equipped with enlarged wheels enabling the fighter to operate from unprepared grass strips. In addition, the main wheel brakes were improved. The bulged tailwheel doors of the MiG-1 were replaced by cutaway doors exposing a portion of the retracted tailwheel.

The MiG-3 retained the Mikulin AM-35A engine, a liquid-cooled supercharged V-12 delivering 1,350 hp at 2,050 rpm for takeoff and nominally rated at 1,130 hp at an altitude of 6,000 meters (19,685 ft). The AM-35A weighed 830 kg (1,830 lb), had a displacement of 46.66 liters (2,847 cu in), and ran on 95-octane fuel. The engine was equipped with four K-35B carburetors and a BS-12 PEA ignition system with two magnetos. The AM-35 was developed from the M-34NBR engine, which in turn had its roots in the M-17, a copy of the German Bavarian Motor Works BMW VI engine.

MiG-3s delivered before summer 1941 were equipped with a VISh-22Ye constant-speed propeller, a Soviet development of an American Hamilton Standard design. The propeller had a diameter of three meters (9.84 feet) and weighed 145 kilograms (320 pounds). However, the majority of all MiG-3s were equipped with a VISh-61Sh three-bladed metal propeller, an indigenous Soviet design, also having a diameter of three meters, and weighing 141 kilograms (311 pounds). The first MiG-3s were equipped with the VISh-61Sh during summer 1941.

▲ An early production MiG-3 during flight evaluation with the *Nauchno-Ispitatel'niy Institut Voyenno-Vozdushikh Sil* (Scientific Research Institute of the Soviet Air Force) at Chalovskaya Air Base. The first production MiG-3s lacked the four blisters on the upper engine cowling which were introduced on subsequent production batches to allow proper function of the two 7.62 mm ShKAS machine guns. The MiG-3 is painted in Factory Green with 'AII' Blue undersurfaces. No national markings have been applied to this particular aircraft. (G. F. Petrov)

MiG-1/MiG-3 Development

MiG-1

Seven cooling slots

No canopy

MiG-3 (Early)

Six slots
Reshaped exhaust shield
Aft-sliding canopy
Cowling blisters
Larger rear window
Redesigned radiator inlet
Repositioned inlet
Access hatch
Enlarged radiator fairing
Exposed tailwheel

The MiG-1 had suffered from frequent engine cooling problems during flight testing. In order to prevent these, the MiG-3's cooling system was improved and an auxiliary oil tank added. The new OP-310 water radiator had a deeper duct and an adjustable exit door.

The dihedral of the outer wing panels was increased from five to six degrees in order to improve stability, and the engine was moved 100 mm (3.9 inches) forward to counterbalance tail heaviness. The engine relocation increased the overall length of the MiG-3 to 8,250 mm (27 ft ¾ in).

Armament, consisting of a centerline-mounted 12.7 mm (.50-caliber) Berezin UBS machine gun with three hundred rounds and two 7.62 mm (.30-caliber) ShKAS machine guns with 375 rounds, was placed above the AM-35A engine. The two ShKAS machine guns were mounted on either side of the Berezin UBS machine gun. The guns were aimed with the aid of a PBP-1A gun sight, a rudimentary lens-type reflector sight with two deflection rings, one for 200 km/h (124 mph) and one for 300 km/h (186 mph).

Armor plate of 8 mm (0.3 in) thickness was installed behind the cockpit, and an additional 250-liter (66 gal) fuel tank was installed under the pilot's seat.

The MiG-3s fuel system was equipped with an automatic fire suppression system, adopted from the LaGG-3, to reduce the risk of fire during maneuvers and combat. Engine exhaust gases were collected from the exhaust manifold and fed to a filter in the rear fuselage and then to the four fuel tanks.

Each MiG-3 had provision for an RSI-3 'Orel' radio transmitter and receiver, with an antenna mast in front of the cockpit offset to starboard and also inclined to starboard. The antenna mast could be removed and usually was fitted only to MiG-3s that were equipped with a radio. The RSI-3 initially was installed on flight commanders' aircraft; remaining MiG-3s were equipped only with a receiver. The short-wave RSI-3 operated on any of five preset frequencies between 3.5 and 5 megahertz.

Unlike earlier Polikarpov I-16 and I-153 fighters, which were equipped with a 12-volt electrical system, the MiG-3 was equipped with a 24-volt electrical system.

The first few production aircraft adopted the same upper engine cowling design from the first MiG-3 (serial number 04). Subsequent production batches had a modified upper engine cowling with an added four 'blisters' in order to allow proper function of the two ShKAS machine guns mounted on top of the engine.

The first MiG-3s (serial number 04) left State Aircraft Factory 1 at Moscow-Khodinka on 29 October 1940, and by New Year's Eve, a total of eleven fighters had been built. Beginning in February 1941, most of these were taken to Ketch airfield on the Crimean peninsula, a region chosen for its mild climate, for combat training and evaluation. Among the experienced pilots flying the MiG-3 was Arkadi N. Yekatov, the first chief test pilot of the MiG Design Bureau, who had performed the maiden flight of the first I-200 prototype. Yekatov's luck ran out on 13 March 1941 when he was killed in the crash of a MiG-3 after losing control of the fighter, which developed severe engine trouble during a high-altitude flight.

State Acceptance Trials with the *NIIVVS* at Chalovskaya Air Base near Moscow took place using two MiG-3s (serial numbers 2107 and 2115) between 27 January and 26 February 1941. Both MiG-3s had been built in December 1940 and were among the first MiG-3s manufactured by State Aircraft Factory 1.

During January 1941, State Aircraft Factory 1 produced a total of 140 new MiG-3s. In April a total of 283 MiG-3 were delivered to various *IAP* (*Istrebitel'niy Aviapolk* — Fighter Aviation Regiments), including eighty sent to units in the Odessa and Kiev Military Districts. This number grew to 394 in May 1941, when 135 MiG-3s were sent to the Leningrad Military District alone. In June 1941, a total of 276 MiG-3s were allocated to operational units. Nearly half of the June production was sent to Fighter Aviation Regiments defending Moscow. (▶ 10)

▼ This early production MiG-3 lacks a canopy. The antenna cable is attached to the starboard side rear fuselage, adjacent to the tactical number. The oil cooler outlet door on the intake fairing is open. The slotted panel located just behind the engine intake fairing is a typical feature for early production MiG-3s. The square aperture in front of the two slots on the starboard upper engine cowling is for the antenna mast. (G.F. Petrov)

▼ Crash landings were only too common with the MiG-3. This early production MiG-3 was equipped with a ski landing gear, as the small ski on the tailwheel indicates. The four blisters on the upper engine cowling are missing, indicating that this is one of the very first MiG-3s produced at State Aircraft Factory 1. Early MiG-3s lacked the wing leading edge slats that were introduced on late production models. (G.F. Petrov)

In summer 1941, the MiG-3 was produced in four shifts around the clock at State Aircraft Factory 1. The average daily output was between fifteen and eighteen fighters, and on some days as many as twenty-six MiG-3s were assembled. During August 1941 a total of 562 MiG-3 were produced, four times as many as in January 1941. Between July and September 1941, no less than 1,508 MiG fighters rolled out of State Aircraft Factory 1.

On 4 July 1941, the State Defense Committee established a special Evacuation Council to supervise the removal of industries to areas behind the Ural Mountains, well beyond the range of the Luftwaffe's bombers. In October 1941, State Aircraft Factory 1 and the MiG Design Bureau were moved to Kuybishev (now Samara) on the Volga River, along with a number of government offices that had been evacuated from Moscow as well. Only a small number of MiG-3s had been built at Kuybishev by the time Soviet leader Josef Stalin personally ordered a halt to MiG-3 production in favor of the Ilyushin Il-2 'Shturmovik' assault aircraft. The last MiG-3 left the assembly line in January 1942. A total of 3,120 MiG-3s were built at State Aircraft Factory 1 within thirteen months, a monthly average of 240 aircraft, or eight MiG-3s per day.

After the return of the MiG Design Bureau from Kuybishev to Khodinka, an additional fifty MiG-3s were assembled from components that had been left behind in Moscow in the chaos of the evacuation. These MiG-3s could be distinguished by their lack of an intake scoop under the engine exhaust stacks on both sides of the nose.

The MiG-3 was of mixed construction. The fuselage comprised two sub-sections joined at four attachment points. The forward portion of the fuselage, from spinner to aft of the cockpit, was of all-metal semimonocoque construction of duralumin panels over a framework of welded steel tubing. The aft portion of the fuselage, which included the vertical fin, was a wooden semimonocoque of four longerons covered with plywood.

The wings of the MiG-3, like the fuselage, were of hybrid construction. The center section was all-metal with a main spar and front and rear auxiliary spars. The outer wing panels were of all-wood construction, each panel having six degrees of built-in dihedral. Wing flaps were all-metal.

Control surfaces were of built-up aluminum frames covered with fabric. The horizontal stabilizers were of wood construction with plywood covering. Both elevators had adjustable trim tabs, and a ground-adjustable trim tab was fitted to the port aileron.

During the course of the production cycle, a number of improvements and changes were made to the MiG-3.

During late spring 1941, the six slots on the panel located behind the oil cooler exhaust door were deleted.

The RSI-3 'Orel' radio was replaced by the more powerful RSI-4 'Malyutka' which operated on variable frequencies in the range of 3.7 to 6.05 megahertz, unlike the five fixed frequencies of the RSI-3. Frequency selection was by means of a knob under the starboard side of the instrument panel.

The thickness of the armor plate aft of the cockpit was increased from 8 mm (0.31 in) to 9 mm (0.35 in) on late production models.

Late MiG-3s differed from early examples in having a lengthened nose. The engine was moved 100 mm (3.9 in) forward in order to eliminate the tail-heavy characteristics of the first production MiG-3s. With this modification, the overall length of the late MiG-3 increased from 8,250 mm (27 ft ¾ in) to 8,350 mm (27 ft 4¾ in).

These late-production MiG-3s also featured a tunnel-shaped cover, over the forward exhaust stack on each side of the engine cowling, which fed cooling air over the three stacks. This was a design feature copied from the Messerschmitt Bf 109E-3 introduced during autumn 1941.

On the port upper engine cowling an additional access hatch was added. To allow easy access to the lower portions of the engine, three flush-mounted snap latches were added to each side of

▼ Late production batches of the MiG-3 were equipped with slats mounted on the wing leading edge and a tunnel-shaped fairing mounted in front of the exhaust stacks, as a result of an evaluation of five Messerschmitt Bf 109E-3s that were purchased by the Soviet government from the Third Reich in May 1940. This particular MiG-3 (serial number 3595) served as a testbed for the Mikulin AM-38 engine. (G.F. Petrov)

▼ A soldier of the German Wehrmacht holds an ammunition belt from the Berezin UBS 12.7 mm machine gun. The two lower fuselage access hatches are open, and the entire engine cowling is missing, exposing the Mikulin AM-35A engine. Lying next to the port main landing gear are bottles of compressed air used to start the engine. Inner surfaces of access panels are natural aluminum. (ECPA DAA 1092 L 24)

Nose Variations

Early MiG-3

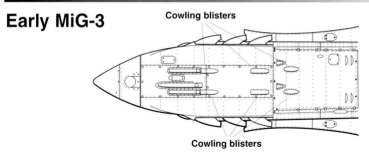

Cowling blisters

Cowling blisters

Late MiG-3

Cover over first exhaust stack

Large fairings

Additional access hatch

Cover over first exhaust stack

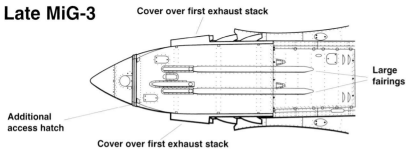

▼ 'White 42' of the 7. *IAP* prepares for an air defense mission over the beleaguered city of Leningrad (now St. Petersburg) during October 1941. The lack of an antenna mast indicates that no radio equipment is installed. The 7th Fighter Aviation Regiment received Guards status on 7 March 1942 and became the 14th Guards Fighter Aviation Regiment. (Klaus Niska)

the lower engine cowling. These latches were also copied from the Messerschmitt Bf 109E-3. On top of the engine cowling, the six blisters mounted over the ShKAS 7.62 mm machine guns were replaced by two long fairings. To make room for the fairings, the two inlets on top of the engine cowlings were slightly repositioned.

A few MiG-3s were equipped with a Hucks-type starter lug on the spinner. Among them were the MiG-3s of the 34. *IAP* .

During the course of production, an improved PBP-1B gun sight replaced the original PBP-1A gun sight.

Late production MiG-3s had a bulged door covering the entire tailwheel, and on some late production batches, tailwheel doors were not fitted at all.

Late production MiG-3s were also equipped with wing leading edge slats. With the addition of slats, the starboard pitot tube was enlarged and relocated under the wing leading edge. The slats were also copied from the Messerschmitt Bf 109E-3 and were introduced on the MiG-3 during autumn 1941.

Strict quality control measures on the production line as well as a much improved surface finish greatly improved the performance of the late production MiG-3. While the first examples had an empty weight of 2,775 kilograms (6,118 lb), this figure was reduced to 2,700 kilograms (5,952 lb) on late production MiG-3s. The maximum speed rose from 608 km/h (378 mph) on early MiG-3s to 640 km/h (398 mph) on late MiG-3s, and service ceiling rose from 11,130 meters (36,516 ft) to 12,050 meters (39,534 ft).

The MiG-3 saw operational service only with the *VVS*. Ironically, the only other countries to fly the MiG-3 during the Great Patriotic War were all enemies of the Soviet Union. The German Luftwaffe evaluated at least three MiG-3s, and a single MiG-3 was test flown by the Aeronautica Regala Romana (Royal Romanian Air Force). (▸▸ 14)

MiG-3 Development

Early Production

Cowling blisters

Uncovered exhaust stack

Inlets

Exposed tailwheel

Late Production

No inlets

Covered exhaust stack

Long fairing

Access hatch

Leading edge slat

Bulged tailwheel door

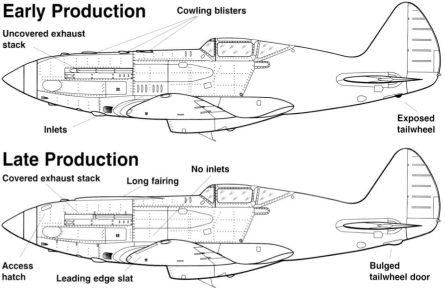

A few operational MiG-3s, like this early production variant, were equipped with the BK gun pod containing a Berezin UB 12.7 mm (.50-caliber) machine gun. The Berezin UB weighed 23.5 kg (52 lb) and was 1,365 mm (54 in) long with a barrel length of 1,010 mm (40 in), and fired seven to eight hundred rounds per minute at a muzzle velocity of 840 m (2,756 ft) per second. It was loaded pneumatically. The six slots in the panel behind the oil cooler exhaust flaps are typical of early production MiG-3s. (G.F. Petrov)

This MiG-3 is equipped with a BK gun pod and a bomb rack under each wing. Part of the upper engine cowling is missing. Mid-production MiG-3s lacked the tunnel-shaped fairing in front of the exhaust stacks, having instead a silver-colored alloy covering. In contrast to the early MiG-3s' slotted panel behind the oil cooler exhaust flap, this particular MiG-3 lacks any slots. No national markings have been applied to its lower wing surfaces. (G.F. Petrov)

▲ The port cockpit of an early MiG-3. On the left side of the upper row of instruments is the cocking handle for the port ShKAS 7.62 mm machine gun. Aft of the machine gun cocking handle are two throttle levers, one for normal cruise, the other for high altitude. On top of the control stick is the brake control lever, and below this is a button for the bomb release mechanism. Inside the control stick grip are the firing buttons for the two ShKAS and the single Berezin UBS machine gun. In the port console is a gauge and control for the oxygen. In front of the control stick the star-shaped knob for the trim control can be seen. The instrument panel is painted black. (Dan Antoniu)

▸ The instrument panel of an early MiG-3. On the upper row are the VD-12 altimeter, the KI-6 compass, the turbocharger indicator, and the BG-4B fuel gauge control. The middle instrument in the upper row is missing. In the middle row are the US-800 speed indicator, the turn-and-bank indicator, the KR-30 variometer, the TE-22 engine tachometer, and the TZT-5 multiple engine instrument. In the lower row are the brake pressure control, the fuel pressure control, the TVE-41 water radiator temperature control, and the TME-41 oil temperature control. The PBP-1A gun sight is installed on a frame above the instrument panel. On the right side of the gun sight is a cushioned crash pad. At top right is the cocking handle for the starboard ShKAS machine gun. The controls of the RSI-4 'Malyutka' radio are on the starboard cockpit wall. The radio operated on frequencies in a band between 3.7 and 6.05 megahertz. (Dan Antoniu)

Underwing Stores

The MiG-1 had no provision for underwing stores, but the MiG-3 had a provision for two bomb racks under each wing. In actual operation, these racks were rarely carried, and in some cases just a single rack was mounted under each wing. Bombs weighing from 8 to 100 kilograms (17.6 to 220 lb) could be carried by the MiG-3. These included the AO-8M, AO-10, or AO-20M3 anti-personnel fragmentation bombs, as well as the FAB-50 and the FAB-100 general purpose bombs. However, the use of the MiG-3 as a fighter-bomber was a rarity during World War II.

By 1940 standards, the armament of the MiG-3 was inferior. To improve it, the BK gun pod, containing a single 12.7 mm Berezin UB machine gun, was introduced. Two of these were carried, one under each wing. These fired outside the propeller disc and needed no synchronization gear. When equipped with the BK gun pods, top speed of the MiG-3 was reduced to 450 km/h (280 mph) at sea level and 589 km/h (366 mph) at an altitude of 7,700 meters (25,262 ft), and service ceiling was reduced to 10,670 meters (35,000 ft). The BK gun pods also adversely affected the handling characteristics of the MiG-3. Only a very few BK gun pod-equipped MiG-3s were deployed to the Western Military Districts before the German attack on the Soviet Union.

The MiG-3 was able to carry a total of six RS-82 (RS: *Raketnij Snarjad* — rocket projectile) unguided air-to-air or air-to-ground missiles. The RS-82 was 560 mm (22 in) long and weighed 6.85 kilograms (15 lb) with a warhead weighing 585 grams (1.3 lb). The range of the RS-82 was 5,200 meters (17,060 ft).

There was also a provision on the MiG-3 for the carriage of two VAP-6M chemical spray dispensers, each containing 38 liters (10 gal) of mustard gas, or two ZAP-6 incendiary spray containers, each containing 14.5 kilograms (32 lb) of granulated phosphorus. Neither were used operationally, although trials of each had been carried out before the war. (▶ 17)

▼ It was a time-consuming process for ground crews to rearm and maintain a MiG-3 because its access panels, unlike those of contemporary aircraft such as the Messerschmitt Bf 109E, were fixed with bolts instead of quick-release latches. In front of the 110-liter (29 US gallons) forward fuselage fuel tank of this MiG-3 is one of the ammunition boxes for the ShKAS 7.62 mm machine guns. The oil cooler outlet flap is nearly closed. (G.F. Petrov)

▲ Armament of the MiG-3 consisted of a centerline-mounted 12.7 mm Berezin UBS machine gun with three hundred rounds and a 7.62 mm ShKAS machine gun with 375 rounds offset to either side, all placed above the engine. Tubular flame dampers were mounted in front of the muzzles of the machine guns. The machine guns fired through the propeller disc and were controlled by a S2K-26 synchronization unit, which was linked by gears to the crankshaft of the Mikulin AM-35A engine. The ammunition feed mechanism was located behind the engine. (G.F. Petrov)

Underwing Stores

RO-82 Rocket Rails

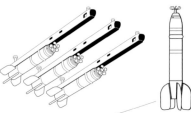

RO-82 unguided rocket

Type BK Gun Pod

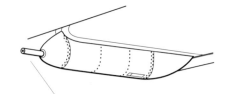

Berezin UB 12.7 mm (.50-cal.) machine gun

VAP-6M Chemical Spray

ZAP-6 Incendiary Spray

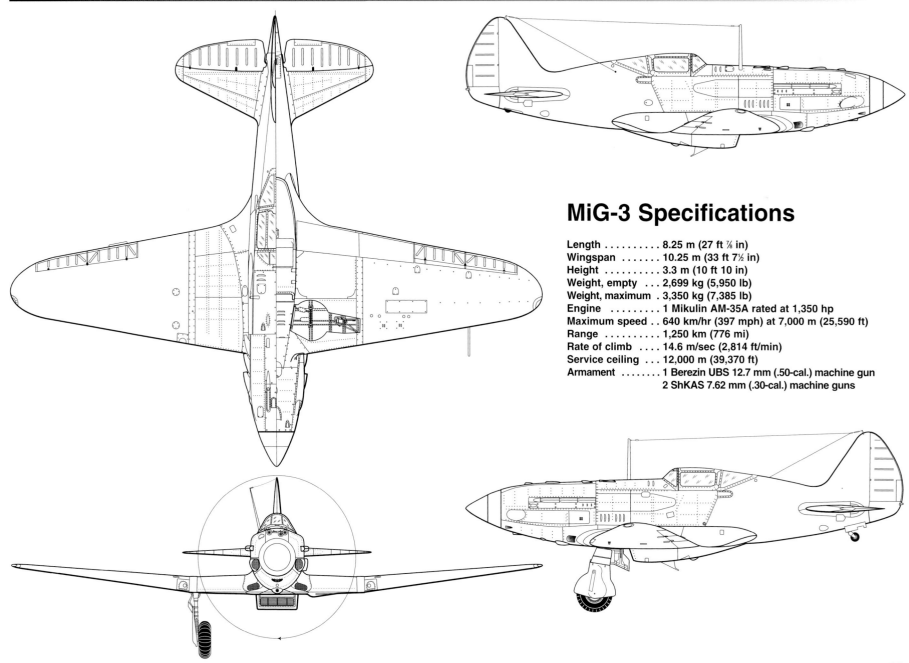

MiG-3 Specifications

Length . . . . 8.25 m (27 ft ⅞ in)
Wingspan . . . . 10.25 m (33 ft 7½ in)
Height . . . . 3.3 m (10 ft 10 in)
Weight, empty . . . 2,699 kg (5,950 lb)
Weight, maximum . 3,350 kg (7,385 lb)
Engine . . . . 1 Mikulin AM-35A rated at 1,350 hp
Maximum speed . . 640 km/hr (397 mph) at 7,000 m (25,590 ft)
Range . . . . 1,250 km (776 mi)
Rate of climb . . . . 14.6 m/sec (2,814 ft/min)
Service ceiling . . . 12,000 m (39,370 ft)
Armament . . . . 1 Berezin UBS 12.7 mm (.50-cal.) machine gun
2 ShKAS 7.62 mm (.30-cal.) machine guns

▲ A freshly delivered Mikulin AM-35A is prepared for installation in a MiG-3. The AM-35A was a V-12 liquid-cooled supercharged engine weighing 830 kg (1,830 lb) and having a displacement of 46.66 liters (2,846 cu in). It used 95-octane fuel and was rated at 1,130 hp at an altitude of 6,000 meters (19,685 ft) and 1,350 hp at 2,050 rpm for takeoff. The engine was equipped with four K-35B carburetors and a BS-12 PEA ignition system with two magnetos. (G.F. Petrov)

▼ The rear fuselage of the MiG-3 was a semimonocoque wooden structure of four pine longerons, pine stringers, and eight hollow frames, each with a Bakelite plywood web. Gusset plates of Bakelite plywood were used at all attachment points. (G.F. Petrov)

▲ A worker assembles the engine cowling of a MiG-3 at State Aircraft Factory 1 at Moscow-Khodinka. Visible are the rectangular openings for the exhaust stacks of the Mikulin AM-35A engine. The engine cowling was painted Factory Green before it was installed on the MiG-3. This was a common procedure at Soviet State Aircraft Factories. (G.F. Petrov)

▼ The rear fuselage skin of the MiG-3 was made of five 0.5 mm thick plywood sheets, and covered on the inside with strips of calico fabric impregnated with a nitrocellulose varnish and on the outside with calico affixed with glue. The entire rear section was painted before mating with the rest of the fuselage; upper surfaces were painted Factory Green and the lower surface 'All' Blue. The color demarcations made by the spray gun varied widely from sharp to soft. (G.F. Petrov)

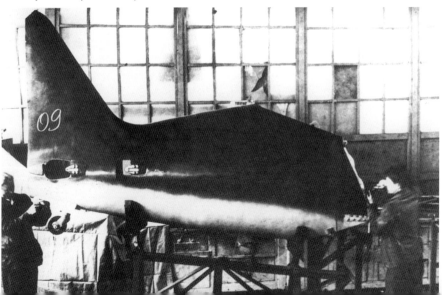

The MiG-3 in Combat

Although the MiG-3 had been developed as a high-altitude interceptor, it was assigned to Frontal Aviation Regiments (tactical fighter squadrons) due to insufficient numbers of other modern Soviet fighters. These units were responsible for the conduct of low-level missions that included ground attack, a duty for which the MiG-3 was not well-suited.

The *IAP* were first equipped with the MiG-3 during April 1941. That month, a total of 247 MiG-3s were distributed to thirteen Regiments. The number of MiG-3s allocated to each Regiment varied widely. For example, the 15. *IAP* based at Kaunas, Lithuania, and the 28. *IAP* at Lvov (formerly Lemberg) in Ukraine each had thirty-nine aircraft on strength, but only four MiG-3s each were distributed to the 4. *IAP* at Kishinev and the 55. *IAP* at Byeltsy in the Odessa Military District on the Black Sea.

The MiG-3 had actually seen combat before the German attack on the Soviet Union (Operation Barbarossa) on 22 June 1941. As a prelude to invasion, the Luftwaffe had, beginning in 1940, performed about five hundred reconnaissance flights over the Soviet Union from bases in Poland, Romania, Bulgaria, and Finland, using Junkers Ju 86P-2s and Ju 88s and Dornier Do 215s of the Aufklärungsgruppe des Oberbefehlshabers der Luftwaffe (Reconnaissance Wing of the Air Force Commander-in-Chief) under the command of Oberstleutnant (Lieutenant Colonel) Theodor Rowehl. Three German aircraft were intercepted and shot down at high altitude by MiG-3s belonging to the 4. *IAP* based at Kishinev in the Odessa Military District. MiG-3s belonging to the 31st Fighter Aviation Regiment tried to intercept a German reconnaissance aircraft over Kaunas, Lithuania, on 10 April 1941, but failed. The information gained by the German reconnaissance crews was a key factor in their initial success in the opening weeks of the war.

At the time of the German attack against the Soviet Union, the MiG-3 was numerically by far the most important new fighter type in the inventory of the Soviet Air Force. Up to the German invasion on 22 June 1941, a total of 1,289 MiG-3s had been produced, but only 399 Yak-1s and 322 LaGG-3s. The MiG-3 therefore represented 37 percent of the total number of operational Soviet fighters, the majority of which were obsolescent Polikarpov I-16s and I-153s. However, of these 1,289 MiG-3s, only 407 of these had been allocated to fully operational Fighter Aviation Regiments in the West. This number rapidly grew to 686 MiG-3s by 1 January 1942.

Most of the MiG-3s assigned to the Western Military Districts were based very close to the borders of the Soviet Union's most probable enemies: the Third Reich and its satellites, such as Romania, Hungary, and Finland. Consequently, Operation Barbarossa took most MiG-3-equipped Fighter Aviation Regiments by complete surprise. Within twenty-four hours, the majority of all MiG-3s assigned to the Western Military Districts had been put out of action. However, there were a few MiG-3s that escaped destruction, and at least a Dornier Do 17 bomber and a Messerschmitt Bf 110 Zerstörer were shot down by MiG-3s.

With its high-altitude performance, the MiG-3 was also assigned to the Regiments of the *PVO* (*Protivovozdushnogo Oborona* — National Air Defense Forces). MiG-3s assigned to *PVO* units were concentrated around the Soviet capital, Moscow, as well as Leningrad (now St. Petersburg) and Baku, the capital of the Azerbaijan Soviet Socialist Republic on the Caspian Sea. The majority of these escaped destruction in the first days of Operation Barbarossa and saw action during Operation Typhoon, the battle for Moscow that started on 30 September 1941. MiG-3s of the *PVO* were frequently engaged against German high-altitude reconnaissance aircraft, such as the Junkers Ju 86P-2, which could fly as high as 12,000 meters (39,370 ft). Khodinka, the birthplace of the MiG-3, also housed MiG-3s of the 6th Fighter Air Corps of the Moscow Air Defense Zone. These fighters defended Moscow from Luftwaffe bombers during 1941 and 1942. (▸ 18)

▾ A line up of MiG-3s of the 12th Guards Fighter Aviation Regiment during the regiment's Guards inauguration ceremony at Vnukovo airfield, Moscow, 7 March 1942. The unit was the former 120th Fighter Aviation Regiment and belonged to the National Air Defense forces assigned to the defense of Moscow. One of its squadron commanders performed the first high-altitude ramming attack when he cut off the tail of a Dornier Do 217 reconnaissance aircraft at an altitude of 9,800 meters (32,152 ft). The MiG-3 nearest camera has the tunnel-shaped fairing in front of the exhaust stacks, a feature typical of late production MiG-3s. However, the fighter lacks another late production feature, the leading edge slats on the wing. (Hans-Joachim Mau)

▾ 'Red 42' was assigned to the Leningrad front during the winter of 1942. The entire MiG-3 was painted in white, including the wing and fuselage undersurfaces and main wheel wells. This is a late production fighter with slats on the wing leading edges and the fairing in front of the exhaust stacks. The red star was applied on the rear fuselage and the tail in accordance with directions issued in late June 1941. A small red star was painted on the white spinner. (G.F. Petrov)

▲ The MiG-3 served well until late 1943. These MiG-3s belonged to the 565. *IAP* of the *Cherno Morskiy Flot* (Black Sea Fleet) and were based at the Kuban front. The national marking has a large white border with a thin red outline, a style introduced in late 1943 that replaced the previous black-outlined red star. No national markings were carried on the upper wing surfaces after June 1941. (G.F. Petrov).

▲ 'White 54' of the 34. *IAP* is unusual in having a Hucks-type starter lug fitted on the propeller hub. Only a very few MiG-3s were so equipped. The MiG-3 carries a camouflage of 'All' Green and 'All' Dark Green on the upper surfaces and 'All' Blue on the lower surfaces. The Black stripes applied in the 'All' Dark Green areas are unusual. The lack of a national insignia on the rear fuselage is not standard for 1943; in late June 1941 a directive was issued that all MiG-3s were to have a red star painted on the rear fuselage as well as the tail. (Robert Bock)

At the beginning of the Great Patriotic War, there was also a small number of MiG-3s assigned to the three Western fleets of the *Aviatsiya Voyenno Morskogo Flota* (Soviet Naval Aviation), and the *Cherno Morskiy Flot* (Black Sea Fleet) had two serviceable MiG-3s when the war began.

Losses of the MiG-3 were mounting to unacceptably high levels during the rapid German advance into the Soviet Union in the summer of 1941, when Major Stepan P. Suprun, a Ukrainian test pilot, suggested the formation of special units equipped with the MiG-3 and consisting only of highly experienced test pilots from the Experimental Design Bureaus, the Flight Research Institute, as well as the Scientific Research Institute of the Air Force.

This idea was quickly approved, and two Special Purpose Fighter Aviation Regiments were established within a few days after the German attack. Major Suprun became the commander of the 401st Special Purpose Fighter Aviation Regiment, which was assigned to the 23rd Mixed Aviation Division and based at Zubovo air field near Smolensk. The Regiment received its baptism of fire on 30 June 1941, and in the first two days of action, Major Suprun shot down a total of eight enemy aircraft. An additional four victories followed, but his luck ran out when he was killed in action near Vitbesk on 4 July 1941. Major Suprun was made a Hero of the Soviet Union posthumously on 22 July 1941, his second such award. The 401st Special Purpose Fighter Aviation Regiment claimed over fifty enemy aircraft shot down before it disbanded in October 1941.

Pyotr M. Stefanovsky, a former test pilot of the *NIIVVS*, became the leader of the 402nd Special Purpose Fighter Aviation Regiment, which was assigned to the Northwestern front. This unit was engaged in the defense of Leningrad (now St. Petersburg). In contrast to the 401st Special Purpose Fighter Aviation Regiment, the 402nd Special Purpose Fighter Aviation Regiment served throughout the entire war and destroyed over eight hundred enemy aircraft. The highly experienced test pilots in the regiment, whose skills were needed for the development and testing of new fighters

as well as improved versions of existing models, were progressively replaced by ordinary pilots. Stefanovsky survived the war and became a deputy chief-designer with the Yakovlev Design Bureau in the rank of Major General.

There were several defects that plagued the few surviving MiG-3s in combat during the summer of 1941. At altitudes above 3,000 meters (9,843 feet), the AM-35A engine suffered from lubrication problems and low fuel pressure, and the pilot's oxygen system frequently malfunctioned. At low and medium altitudes, where most of the combat on the Eastern front was performed, the MiG-3 did not perform very well. Combat experience showed that the Yak-1s and LaGG-3s, with their Klimov M-105 engines, were by far better suited for this kind of operation. When sufficient numbers of these two fighter types became available in early 1944, most of the remaining MiG-3s were retired from front-line service. However, MiG-3s remained in service with the *PVO* until the end of World War II and were the principal fighter for the around-the-clock defense of Moscow.

A number of future Soviet aces claimed their first kills in MiG-3s, including Aleksandr I. Pokryshkin, who with fifty-nine personal victories was the second highest-ranking ace of the Soviet Air Force. At the beginning of the war, Senior Lieutenant Aleksandr I. Pokryshkin was assigned to the 55. *IAP*, based at Mayaki airstrip in Soviet-occupied Moldavia. The first aircraft he shot down on the first day of war in his MiG-3 was actually a Sukhoi Su-2 dive bomber, a new type in the Soviet inventory which he and his comrades mistook for an enemy aircraft. A day later, he downed a genuine German aircraft near Jassy. Pokryshkin claimed most of his later victories while flying Lend-Lease Bell P-39 Airacobras. Major Evgraf Ryzow of the 32. *IAP* claimed nineteen victories, six of them shared with other pilots. Lieutenant K.S. Alekseev of the 910. *IAP* of the National Air Defense Forces had ten victories to his credit and became a Hero of the Soviet Union.

Lieutenant Aleksey N. Katrisht, Squadron Leader in the 20. *IAP* of the *PVO*, became the first Soviet pilot to perform a ramming attack at high altitude. During the night of 21-22 September 1941, he was briefed to intercept a Dornier Do 217 high-altitude reconnaissance aircraft proceeding towards Moscow at an altitude of 9,800 meters (32,152 ft). Having exhausted his ammunition supply, he rammed the Do 217, damaging its two horizontal stabilizers with the propeller of his MiG-3. The German aircraft went into a spin and crashed, while Katrisht was able to land his MiG-3 with minor damage. For this action, Katrisht became a Hero of the Soviet Union on 28 October 1941. His unit, the 20th Fighter Aviation Regiment became the 12th Guards Fighter Aviation Regiment on 7 March 1942. During the Great Patriotic War, Katrisht shot down a further fourteen enemy aircraft. In the early 1980s, he became a Colonel-General and Deputy Supreme Commander of the Warsaw Pact Air Forces in Europe.

MiG-3 Camouflage and Markings

MiG-3s manufactured before the German invasion in summer 1941 were delivered with upper surfaces in either Factory Green (approximately FS595b: 24058), a unique color only applied to MiG-3s built at State Aircraft Factory 1, or *AII* Green (FS595b: 24258), with undersurfaces painted *AII* Blue (FS595b: 25466). A number of MiG-3s were delivered in a two-color scheme which used *AII* Green and *AII* Black (FS595b: 27038) on upper surfaces with *AII* Blue undersurfaces. Delivery of these two-color MiG-3s started in late spring of 1941.

The *AII* Green and *AII* Black scheme was the principal camouflage pattern for MiG-3s produced after the German attack. A few MiG-3s were also painted in *AII* Green and *AII* Dark Green (FS595b: 24066) with *AII* Blue undersurfaces. Some MiG-3s returned from repair shops having their original *AII* Green upper surfaces mottled by *AII* Dark Green.

During the first winter (1941-42) of the war, the MiG-3 received a winter camouflage of white upper surfaces. A number of MiG-3s received the white camouflage on the production line, while others were painted white in the field or at front-line repair shops. Most winter-camouflaged MiG-3s retained their *AII* Blue undersurfaces, but some MiG-3s were painted entirely in white. The white paint normally used was made of casein and was easily soiled and wore badly.

Most of the inner surfaces of engine cowling panels and access hatches of the MiG-3 were left in natural aluminum. The majority of MiG-3s had instrument panels painted either in black or aluminum. Propeller spinners were painted either *AII* Black, *AII* Green, or Factory Green. The propeller blades were either painted *AII* Black or left in natural aluminum. Main wheel wells and inner surfaces of main wheel doors were painted *AII* Blue. Wheel hubs were usually *AII* Black.

The national marking, a red star with a thin black outline, was applied on the upper and lower wing surfaces and rear fuselage of all MiG-3s leaving State Aircraft Factory 1 until late June 1941. A number of different shades of red, ranging from vermillion to a red-brown, were used for the star. These shades were similar to FS595b: 21105, 21136, or 21302. Aircraft built after June 1941 received an additional red star on the tail. Beginning in mid-1942, a white border began to replace the black border of the national marking. This border was thin at first but gradually became wider as the war progressed.

At the time of the German invasion, most MiG-3s deployed in the Western Military Districts lacked any tactical markings. However, during the course of the war, a variety of two- and three-digit tactical numbers came to be used on the MiG-3, usually painted in red, yellow, or white in front of the national marking on the fuselage. MiG-3s belonging to the 401st Special Purpose Fighter Aviation Regiment had large two-digit white tactical numbers painted over the entire tail. (▶ 20)

▾ This MiG-3 captured by the Third Reich was painted with full Luftwaffe markings. The outer wing, engine cowling, and spinner were painted yellow. After trials with the Luftwaffe, the MiG-3 became part of a sample collection exhibited to the German public in various locations throughout the Third Reich. (Jet & Prop Magazine via Heinz Birkholz)

▾ A MiG-3 on exhibit at Beutepark 5 der Luftwaffe (War Booty Depot 5 of the Air Force) at La Folie-Nanterre near the French capital of Paris. The Luftwaffe referred to the type by its military designation 'I-200' and not the public designation 'MiG-3.' The MiG-3 was destroyed in September 1944 during heavy fighting between Free French forces and the retreating German Wehrmacht. The Polikarpov I-153 in the background, however, survived the war and is now part of the Musée de l'Air. (Bundesarchiv Koblenz)

▲ A Ukrainian pilot defected with this MiG-3 on 3 December 1941, landing at Melitopol in the Ukraine, an airfield occupied by the Escadrila de Observatie 19 (19th Reconnaissance Squadron) of the Aeronautica Regala Romana (Royal Romanian Air Force). The vertical stiffener on the main wheel cover door clearly denotes an early production model of the MiG-3. The MiG-3 is painted in Factory Green with 'All' Blue undersurfaces. One of the squadron's IAR-39 biplanes is visible in the background. (Dan Antoniu)

▼ A Romanian officer of the Escadrila de Observatie 19 poses in front of the captured MiG-3. Unusual for a Soviet fighter, there was a bomb rack fitted on each wing. No tactical number was carried by the MiG-3, which was flown to Brasov (Kronstadt) for further evaluation, escorted by two IAR-80 fighters. (Dan Antoniu)

German MiG-3s

In the first days of the German attack on the Soviet Union, a large number of MiG-3s were captured and taken to German war booty depots. Some of these fighters were shipped to Germany for further investigation at various institutions in the Third Reich. At least three MiG-3s saw service with the German Luftwaffe, and a late production MiG-3 was evaluated at the Test and Evaluation Center of the Luftwaffe at Rechlin.

Components of MiG-3s captured on the Eastern front were sent to the DVL (Deutsche Versuchsanstalt für Luftfahrt — German Research Institute for Aviation) at Berlin-Adlershof, where they were carefully dismantled and analyzed. Based on this research, a number of technical reports were published and distributed throughout the technical departments of the Luftwaffe as well as to the aircraft manufacturers of the Third Reich.

The huge numbers of weapons captured by Germany on the Eastern front were soon revealed to the public at exhibitions in a number of cities of the Third Reich. A single MiG-3 was taken to the sample collection located in the Beutepark 5 der Luftwaffe (War Booty Depot 5 of the Air Force) at La Folie-Nanterre near the French capital of Paris. However, the MiG-3 was destroyed in September 1944 during heavy ground combat in the vicinity of the depot.

The number of MiG-3s captured in the early days of Operation Barbarossa was so huge that the Third Reich entertained a proposal to sell some of them to Finland, one of Germany's allies. Twenty-two nearly new MiG-3s without armament and radios were ordered by the Finnish government, and a unit price of thirty thousand Reichsmarks was agreed upon by both countries. In desperate need of hard currency, the Third Reich sought payment of 220,000 US dollars instead of Reichmarks. It was finally agreed that the aircraft would be handed over on 20 March 1943, but the Third Reich subsequently informed Finland that all MiG-3s destined for that country had become victims of a Soviet bombing raid. As a result, the Finnish Air Force operated no MiG-3s during World War II.

The Romanian MiG-3

On 3 December 1941, a MiG-3 approached Melitopol, a city in the southern Ukraine on the Molochnaya River. The Soviet fighter descended to a former Soviet airbase occupied by Romanian Forces, lowered its landing gear, touched down, and taxied in. Believing it was a Romanian fighter plane, the soldiers of the Escadrila de Observatie 19 (19th Reconnaissance Squadron) of the Aeronautica Regala Romana (Royal Romanian Air Force) did not take much notice of the aircraft. But when they spotted the red star on the MiG-3, the Romanians initially did not trust their eyes. The MiG-3 was flown by a defecting Ukrainian Lieutenant, who had taken off that morning from Perekop, in Crimea, on a mission to escort Soviet bombers. He had selected Melitopol because he was familiar with the airfield from previous exercises.

For further investigation the MiG-3 was flown from Melitopol airfield to the Industria Aeronautica Romana (Romanian Aeronautical Industry) at Brasov (Kronstadt). The IAR works at Brasov (Kronstadt) was the center of the Romanian aviation industry, and its engineers and specialists were eager to examine the latest fighter type in the inventory of the Soviet Air Force. The MiG-3 was flown by a number of pilots, including the Romanian Air Force's top ace, Capitan Aviator de Rezerva (Captain) Constantin M. "Bazu" Cantacuzino.

On 23 August 1944, Romania ceased hostilities against the Allies and requested an armistice, under the terms of which the Romanian Air Force was required to return the captured aircraft to its rightful owner. The only MiG-3 to ever serve in the Romanian Air Force was handed over to the Red Army in early September 1944.

(▶▶ 22)

▲ The MiG-3 was flown at Brasov (Kronstadt) by a number of pilots, including the Romanian Air Force's top ace, Capitan Aviator de Rezerva (Reserve Captain) Constantin M. 'Bazu' Cantacuzino, commander of the Grupul Vanatoare 9 (9th Fighter Group). Cantacuzino, who shot down a total of fifty-six enemy aircraft during World War II, had been Romania's pre-war champion aerobatic pilot. He survived the war and emigrated to Spain after the end of the hostilities in Europe. (Dan Antoniu)

▼ The MiG-3 during its evaluation trials with the Industria Aeronautica Romana (Romanian Aeronautical Industry) at Brasov (Kronstadt). The fronts of the propeller blades are painted silver, while most of the rear of each blade is painted black. A large portion of the wing tip is painted yellow, and a yellow stripe has been added on the rear fuselage. (Dan Antoniu)

▲ The MiG-3 during its evaluation trials at Brasov (Kronstadt). This location was the center of the Romanian aviation industry, whose engineers and specialists were eager to examine the latest fighter in the inventory of the Soviet Air Force. (Dan Antoniu)

▼ The large white '2' painted on the vertical fin denotes that the MiG-3 was the second Soviet aircraft to be captured by Romanian forces (the first was a Polikarpov I-16 Type 29). The white 'E.19' above the tactical number refers to the unit — the Escadrila de Observatie 19 (19th Reconnaissance Squadron) — that had captured the Soviet fighter. (Dan Antoniu)

I-230 (MiG-3U)

▲ The I-230 was an aerodynamically cleaner derivative of the MiG-3. The first prototype of the I-230 (serial number D-1) took off for its maiden flight at Kuibyshev on 31 May 1943 with Viktor Nikitovich Savkin at the controls. The plane was powered by an AM-35A engine, taken from a MiG-3, turning an AV-5L-126A propeller. The first prototype of the I-230 lacked an antenna mast. The national markings had a thin white outline. (Robert Bock)

▼ During a test flight, one of the pre-production I-230s suffered an engine failure which left oil splattered and streaked on the fuselage and the canopy. In contrast to the first prototype, this aircraft had an antenna mast and was in an overall silver finish. (Robert Bock)

The I-230 was the result of a requirement issued by the *NKAP* on 27 February 1943 for a modern interceptor for the *PVO*. The new fighter was to have a speed of around 670 km/h (416 mph) and a service ceiling of 12,500 meters (41,010 ft). It also was to be built of commonly available materials, in order to reduce the quantities of light metals required. Aluminum and other light alloys were in short supply in the Soviet Union immediately following the German attack on 22 June 1941, and Lend-Lease deliveries of such metals from the United States had not yet begun. Accordingly, the successor to the MiG-3 was to be made of wood. Designated 'D' by the MiG Design Bureau, the new fighter received the military designation 'I-230' and the public designation 'MiG-3U.'

The general lines of the I-230 were similar to those of the well-proven MiG-3. With a length of 8.62 meters (28 ft 3⅜ in), the MiG-3U was 370 mm (14½ inches) longer than the MiG-3. This modification was introduced to allow the installation of a 440-liter (116-gal) fuel tank behind the engine. The I-230 was extremely clean aerodynamically, with few of the fairings and blisters found on the MiG-3, and the design of the MiG-3U was such that it could be easily manufactured on the existing MiG-3 production lines.

As no new high-altitude engine was available for the new fighter, the MiG Design Bureau had to rely on the Mikulin AM-35A. The three large exhaust stacks on either side were replaced by six exhaust stubs, and the large exhaust shield of the MiG-3 was replaced by a small square plate. The I-230's under-fuselage radiator fairing was reduced in size. The intake for the oil cooler was deleted from both sides of the nose. A new canopy improved the view for the pilot.

The complex undercarriage of the MiG-3 was modified and became more reliable as a result. Instead of a single main landing gear door, the I-230 had a two-piece cover. The I-230 had two position lights fitted on top and bottom of each wing tip instead of the single light of the MiG-3. A large access hatch was added on the port side of the fuselage.

The first prototype of the I-230 (serial number D-1) took off for its maiden flight at Kuibyshev on 31 May 1943 with Viktor Nikitovich Savkin at the controls. The plane was powered by an AM-35A engine taken from a MiG-3. The engine drove an AV-5L-126A propeller.

The I-230 was the first fighter developed by the MiG Design Bureau to be equipped with cannon armament, in keeping with a trend away from small-caliber weapons, such as the ShKAS 7.62 mm machine gun, which were no longer very effective against all-metal German aircraft. Two synchronized ShVAK 20 mm (.78-caliber) cannons were mounted above the engine of the I-230, and an ammunition supply of 150 rounds per cannon was provided. The ShVAK (*Shpitalny-Vladimirova Aviatsionnaya Krupnokalibernaya* — Shpitalny-Vladimirov large caliber cannon) was developed by Boris G. Shpitalny and S.V. Vladimirov from the highly successful 7.62 mm ShKAS machine gun and became available in 1936. It had an overall length of 1,760 mm (69 in), weighed 42 kg (93 lb), and had a rate of fire of 750 to 800 rounds per minute. A PBP-1A gun sight was installed in the cockpit. The radio equipment included an RSI-4 '*Malyutka*' which was also installed in the MiG-3.

The I-230 prototype was followed by a batch of five pre-production MiG-3Us (serial numbers D-02 to D-06). These I-230s differed from the prototype in having a radio antenna mast and a slightly enlarged under-fuselage radiator fairing. The wing span was enlarged from 10.2 meters (33 ft 5½ in) to 11 meters (36 ft 1 in). The MiG-3U had a top speed of 660 km/h (410 mph) at an altitude of 6,000 meters (19,685 ft), a rate of climb of 13.4 m/sec (2,646 ft/min), a service ceiling of 12,000 meters (39,370 ft), and a range of 1,350 kilometers (839 miles).

The pre-production I-230s were allocated for operational testing to the 12th Guards Fighter Aviation Regiment, which was at the time involved in heavy fighting over the Kalinin front northwest of Moscow. The 12th Guards Fighter Aviation Regiment was the former 20th Fighter Aviation Regiment, which had received Guards status on 7 March 1943. The unit was under the command of Lt. Col. A. S. Pisanko.

The combat evaluation of the MiG-3U showed the superiority of cannon armament over small caliber machine guns. But in the meantime, problems had arisen that killed the prospect for any future mass production of the MiG-3U. In January 1943 the production of the AM-35A engine was switched to the AM-38F, which was specially developed for the Ilyushin Il-2 'Shturmovik.' The Il-2 had to operate at ground level, where high-altitude qualities were not demanded. In addition, the AM-38F ran on low-octane fuel as used by military trucks, unlike the AM-35A, which instead required 95-octane fuel. For these reasons, the AM-38F was not suited for fighter service.

In addition to the lack of a suitable engine, there was also no State Aircraft Factory available at the time with the capacity for production of the MiG-3U. The aircraft was accordingly cancelled.

I-231

When it became clear that the AM-35A engine intended for the I-230 would no longer be available, the MiG Design Bureau began desperately looking for a suitable substitute. During 1942, the Design Bureau of Aleksandr A. Mikulin had developed the new AM-39, which had an output of 1,800 hp at takeoff and 1,300 hp at an altitude of 7,100 meters (23,294 ft), a considerable boost in performance over the AM-38A. The first AM-39 became available to the MiG Design Bureau during September 1943.

The new fighter with the AM-39 received the MiG Experimental Designation '2D' and the military designation 'I-231.' Other than the engine, the major difference between the I-230 and I-231 was in the construction of the fuselage. The wood fuselage of the I-230 was replaced by a metal semimonocoque fuselage on the I-231. The I-231 was armed with two ShVAK 20 mm cannons placed above the engine. Ammunition supply was 160 rounds per gun, ten rounds per gun more than the I-230. The I-231 had the same wing span as the I-230 prototype.

The sole I-231 prototype took off for the first time on 19 October 1943 with Viktor Nikitovich Savkin at the controls. Performance of the I-231 was very impressive for contemporary Soviet fighter standards. It had a maximum speed of 707 km/h (439 mph) at 7,100 meters (23,294 ft), 47 km/h (29 mph) faster than the I-230. Its rate of climb was 18.5 m/sec (3,645 ft/min) and its service ceiling was 11,400 meters (37,402 ft). During a flight on 5 November 1943, the supercharger on the AM-39 disintegrated. Factory tests resumed on 23 November 1943 after repairs.

The I-231 was assigned for State Acceptance Trials on 26 February 1944. Before this transfer took place, the initial AV-5L-126A propeller was exchanged for a AV-5L-126Ye propeller. During the State Acceptance Trials, the prototype was damaged on 8 March 1944 in a landing accident. Test pilot Pyotr M. Stefanovsky survived the crash, and the prototype was repaired. The I-231 returned to the trials on 12 May 1944. An engine malfunction was recorded during a flight on 19 May 1944 and the I-231 was grounded for investigation.

When it became clear that the AM-39 would not be mass-produced, the I-231 program was cancelled in late May 1944 due to the lack of a suitable substitute engine. In addition, there was no production capacity available, as the Yakovlev and Lavochkin fighters were well-established on the production lines of the State Aircraft Factories by late spring 1944, and there was no reason to interrupt their production.

The I-231 was the last derivative of the MiG-3 fighter to be developed. (▸▸ 24)

▲ The I-230 was the first MiG fighter to be equipped with cannon armament. The five pre-production I-230s were assigned to the 12th Guards Fighter Aviation Regiment and took part in operations at the Kalinin front in 1943. The 12th was the former 20th Fighter Aviation Regiment which had received its Guards status on 7 March 1943. The tip of the rudder as well as the wing tips and the front half of the spinner are painted white. (Robert Bock)

▼ The I-231, powered by an AM-39 experimental engine, was the last derivative of the MiG-3. The sole I-231 prototype took off for the first time on 19 October 1943 piloted by Viktor Nikitovich Savkin. During State Acceptance Trials, with Pyotr M. Stefanovsky at the controls, it was damaged in a landing accident on 8 March 1944 and subsequently repaired. (Robert Bock)

I-220 (MiG-11)

In late 1942, the MiG Design Bureau began the development of a high-altitude fighter. Soviet experience showed that most air combat with the German Luftwaffe occurred at low and medium levels, and the Yakovlev and Lavochkin fighters performed this task well. However, at that time the Soviet Union lacked a high-altitude fighter able to catch the Junkers Ju 86P-2 and Ju 86R-1 high-altitude reconnaissance aircraft that frequently intruded into Soviet airspace. Even before the beginning of the war, Ju 86P-2s under the command of Lieutenant Colonel Theodor Rowehl had taken excellent photos of advanced airfields in the Soviet Union. The information contained in these photos was one of the key factors in the Luftwaffe's destruction of 1,489 Soviet fighters and bombers on the ground on the first day of Operation Barbarossa.

The Junkers Ju 86P-2 and Ju 86R-1 that flew through Soviet skies at altitudes of 12,000 meters (39,370 ft) were regarded as a real threat by *Stavka* (*Shtab Glavnovo Verkhovnovo Kommandovaniya* — Headquarters, Supreme High Command). A requirement for a high altitude fighter had been issued by the *NKAP* before the German attack in early 1941, at a time when the clandestine German overflights were observed in increasing number, but due to the chaos of the first months of the war, it was not until late 1942 that work on two prototypes of such a high-altitude fighter was begun.

In contrast to earlier designs having their roots in the MiG-3, the new type was entirely new. Its wing was manufactured of wood and duralumin, its tail of light alloy. The fuel tanks were bladders made of rubberized fabric with a self-sealing coating. The new type received the MiG Design Bureau designation 'A' and the Soviet military designation 'I-220.' The public designation 'MiG-11' was allocated to the high-altitude fighter.

Armament consisted of two ShVAK 20 mm cannons placed above the engine, with an ammunition supply of 150 rounds each. It was intended to use the powerful AM-39 engine in the new fighter, but this was not ready when the prototype was finished, so the proven 1,700 hp AM-38F that powered the Il-2 'Sturmovik' was chosen. The first prototype (serial number 01) left the experimental shop of the MiG Design Bureau at Moscow-Khodinka in September 1942 for ground taxiing trials and took off for the first time on 26 December 1942 with Aleksey P. Yakimov at the controls. The I-220 had a maximum speed of 630 km/h (391 mph) at an altitude of 7,000 meters (22,966 ft). Service ceiling was 9,500 meters (31,168 ft), some 2,500 meters (8,202 ft) below that of the German Junkers Ju 86 spy planes.

In April 1943, the first I-220 was re-engined with the AM-39, which offered 1,800 hp at takeoff. The empty weight of the modified I-220 rose from 2,936 kilograms (6,473 lb) to 3,013 kilograms (6,642 lb). In tests, the modified I-220 attained a top speed of 668 km/h (415 mph), 38 km/h (24 mph) faster than the AM-38F-powered version. Severe problems with the AM-39 led to reinstallation of the original AM-38F engine. Tests with the AM-38F-equipped I-220 started on 1 October 1943, but a day later, the prototype suffered a landing accident and was not repaired until late October 1943. The I-220 was modified again in March 1944, receiving an AM-39 engine and four ShVAK 20 mm cannons, each with an ammunition supply of one hundred rounds.

The second prototype (serial number 02) was available in early 1944. It was equipped from the beginning with the AM-39 engine and four ShVAK cannons, two above the engine and one on either side. The second prototype of the I-220 attained a speed of 697 km/h (433 mph) at an altitude of 7,000 meters and a rate of climb of 22 m/sec (4,374 ft/min), but its service ceiling of 11,000 meters (36,089 ft) was still 1,000 meters (3,280 ft) below that of the German high altitude reconnaissance aircraft it was designed to intercept. This performance deficit, plus the unreliability of the AM-39 engine, led to the cancellation of the I-220 project. The second prototype of the I-220 was subsequently rebuilt into the I-225 interceptor prototype.

(▸ 27)

▼ **The first prototype of the I-220 was initially powered by an AM-38F engine that was subsequently replaced by an AM-39. The I-220 was the first prototype of a series of high-altitude fighters developed by the MiG Design Bureau. The first I-220 did not carry an antenna mast. (G.F. Petrov)**

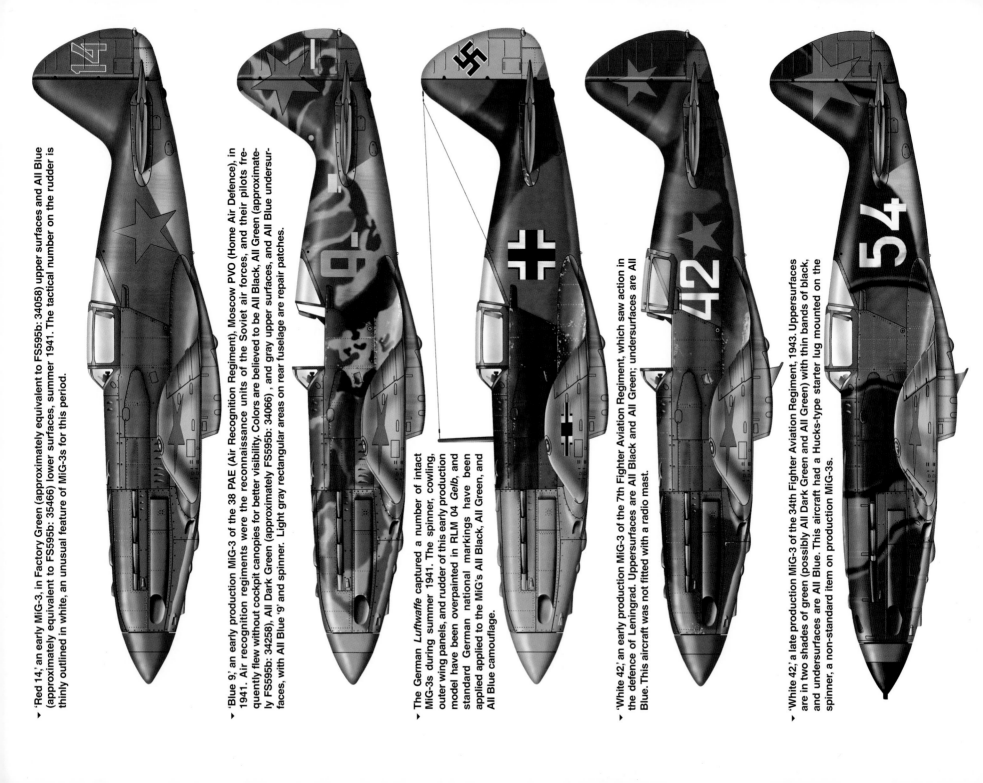

▶ 'Red 14,' an early MiG-3, in Factory Green (approximately equivalent to FS595b: 34058) upper surfaces and All Blue (approximately equivalent to FS595b: 35466) lower surfaces, summer 1941. The tactical number on the rudder is thinly outlined in white, an unusual feature of MiG-3s for this period.

▶ 'Blue 9,' an early production MiG-3 of the 38 PAE (Air Recognition Regiment), Moscow PVO (Home Air Defence), in 1941. Air recognition regiments were the reconnaissance units of the Soviet air forces, and their pilots frequently flew without cockpit canopies for better visibility. Colors are believed to be All Black, All Green (approximately FS595b: 34258), All Dark Green (approximately FS595b: 34066), and gray upper surfaces, and All Blue undersurfaces, with All Blue '9' and spinner. Light gray rectangular areas on rear fuselage are repair patches.

▶ The German *Luftwaffe* captured a number of intact MiG-3s during summer 1941. The spinner, cowling, outer wing panels, and rudder of this early production model have been overpainted in RLM 04 *Gelb*, and standard German national markings have been applied to the MiG's All Black, All Green, and All Blue camouflage.

▶ 'White 42,' an early production MiG-3 of the 7th Fighter Aviation Regiment, which saw action in the defence of Leningrad. Uppersurfaces are All Black and All Green; undersurfaces are All Blue. This aircraft was not fitted with a radio mast.

▶ 'White 42,' a late production MiG-3 of the 34th Fighter Aviation Regiment, 1943. Uppersurfaces are in two shades of green (possibly All Dark Green and All Green) with thin bands of black, and undersurfaces are All Blue. This aircraft had a Hucks-type starter lug mounted on the spinner, a non-standard item on production MiG-3s.

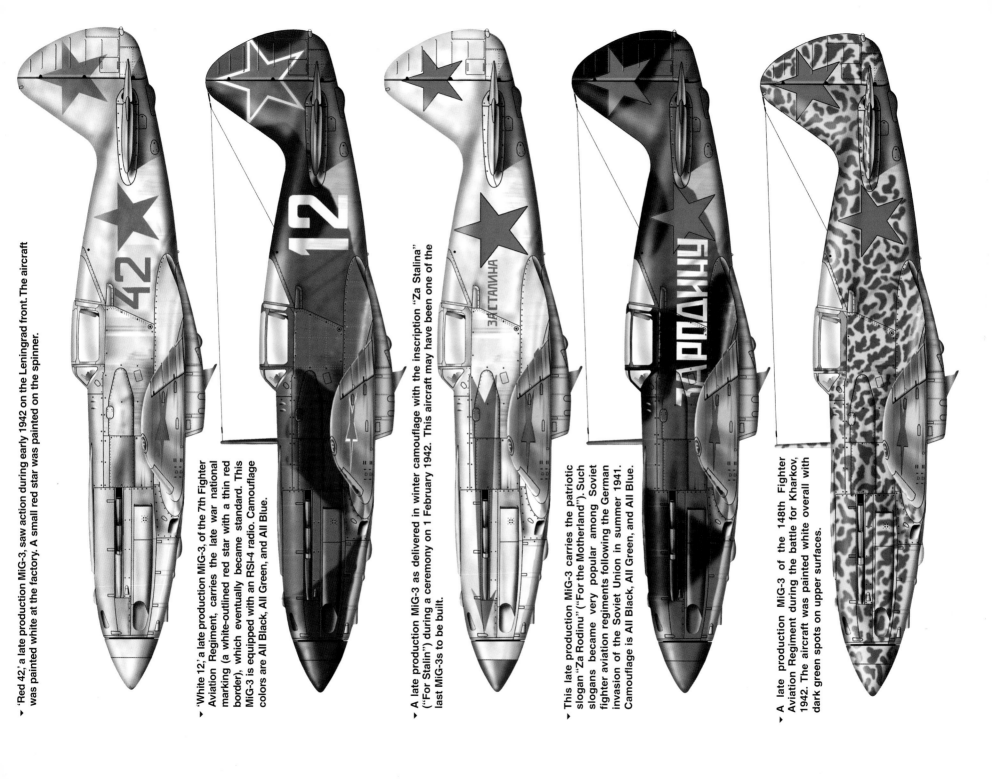

▶ 'Red 42,' a late production MiG-3, saw action during early 1942 on the Leningrad front. The aircraft was painted white at the factory. A small red star was painted on the spinner.

▶ 'White 12,' a late production MiG-3, of the 7th Fighter Aviation Regiment, carries the late war national marking (a white-outlined red star with a thin red border), which eventually became standard. This MiG-3 is equipped with an RSI-4 radio. Camouflage colors are All Black, All Green, and All Blue.

▶ A late production MiG-3 as delivered in winter camouflage with the inscription "Za Stalina" ("For Stalin") during a ceremony on 1 February 1942. This aircraft may have been one of the last MiG-3s to be built.

▶ This late production MiG-3 carries the patriotic slogan "Za Rodinu" ("For the Motherland"). Such slogans became very popular among Soviet fighter aviation regiments following the German invasion of the Soviet Union in summer 1941. Camouflage is All Black, All Green, and All Blue.

▶ A late production MiG-3 of the 148th Fighter Aviation Regiment during the battle for Kharkov, 1942. The aircraft was painted white overall with dark green spots on upper surfaces.

I-222 (MiG-7)

The I-222 high-altitude fighter was a derivative of the I-220 equipped with a pressurized cockpit. The MiG Design Bureau designation was '3A,' and its public designation was 'MiG-7.' The I-222 was powered by an AM-39B-1 engine with an output of 1,760 hp. The engine was equipped with an TK-2B supercharger on its port side, and an intercooler was located under the front fuselage on the centerline. The I-222 had an empty weight of 3,167 kilograms (6,982 lb) and was armed with two ShVAK cannons, one mounted low on each side of the engine.

The I-222 was initially equipped with an AV-5L three-blade propeller, but was subsequently modified with a four-bladed AV-9L-230 propeller specially developed for high altitudes. The forward fuselage was deepened to provide space for the duct connecting the engine exhaust to the exhaust-driven supercharger. The fuselage aft of the cockpit was glazed, affording the pilot a better rear view than on the I-220, and a small air inlet was mounted on the canopy frame. The pilot was protected by a bullet-proof windshield and armor plates behind the seat.

The I-222 made its maiden flight on 7 May 1944. With the supercharged engine, the high-altitude performance of the I-222 was superior to that of the I-220. Its ceiling of 11,300 meters (37,073 ft) approached that of the Junkers Ju 86R-1. It even reached an altitude of 12,000 meters (39,370 ft) during one of its test flights, but at this altitude the engine started to malfunction. Evaluation took place until January 1945, when the engine was returned to Factory 300 for further development. It was refitted to the I-222 in July 1945, but a loss of oil pressure hampered further flying.

The I-222 would have been the perfect high-altitude interceptor at the time of the German attack on the Soviet Union in 1941, but by the time it became available three years later, there was no longer any threat of German high altitude reconnaissance aircraft flying over Soviet territory. The project was quietly phased out in late summer 1945. (▶▶ 28)

▲ The I-222, in its original configuration with an AV-5L three-blade propeller, lacks any camouflage and national markings. The I-222 was first flown on 7 May 1944 with Aleksandr I. Zhukov at the controls. It completed a total of thirty-nine factory test flights. (G.F. Petrov)

▼ The modified I-222 was equipped with an AV-9L-230 four-blade propeller. The fuselage immediately behind the exhaust of the TK-2B supercharger was deepened, and a small inlet was mounted on the canopy frame. With a maximum ceiling of 11,300 meters (37,073 ft), the I-222 was equal in altitude performance to the Junkers Ju 86 R-1 spyplane. (G.F. Petrov)

I-224 (MiG-7)

The I-224 was the last design of the MiG Design Bureau for a high-altitude fighter. The plane received the MiG Design Bureau designation '4A' and the public designation 'MiG-7.'

The I-224 had a pressurized cockpit made of welded dural sheet. The cockpit was air-conditioned and fitted with an inflatable seal. Cockpit pressurization was provided by the supercharger compressor.

The I-224 differed in a number of details from its predecessor, the I-222. The conical spinner on the I-222 was replaced by a pointed spinner. The I-224 was driven by an AV-9L-26B propeller with four wide-chord (400 mm — 15¾ in) blades, specially developed by the *Tsentral'niy Institut Aviatsionnovo Motorstoeniya* (Central Aviation Engine Institute) for high altitudes. The I-222 used an AV-9L-230 propeller with narrow blades.

On the I-224, the TK-300B turbo-supercharger was fitted on the starboard side instead of the port side as on the I-222. The intercooler, placed on the centerline under the fuselage, was enlarged, and its housing was aerodynamically refined. Two exhausts for the engine radiator were place on the upper wing. These outlets were not fitted on the I-222.

The I-224, like the I-222, was armed with two 20 mm ShVAK cannons. Their locations remained unchanged, but the cannon ports were slightly modified.

The I-224 took off for its maiden flight on 20 October 1944 with Aleksey P. Yakimov at the controls. Its maximum speed of 693 km/h (431 mph) was 11 km/h (7 mph) faster than that of the I-222. During one of the few factory test flights the I-224 reached an altitude of 14,100 meters (46,260 feet).

The I-224 suffered from many problems, especially with the TK-300B turbo-supercharger, and as a result was never submitted for State Acceptance Trials. All factory trials of the single I-224 prototype were stopped on 30 November 1946.

▲ While the I-222 carried its supercharger on the port side, that of the I-224 was installed on the starboard side. The I-224's gun ports on the engine cowling also were modified, and its pitot tube was directly attached to the wing leading edge. The I-224 was painted light gray on its upper surfaces and light blue on its undersurfaces. The national markings had a white border with a thin red outline. (G.F. Petrov)

▼ The I-224 had its TK-300B supercharger mounted on the starboard side. On the port side, conventional exhaust stubs were used. The I-224 flew for the first time on 20 October 1944 with Aleksey P. Yakimov at the controls. Its maximum speed of 693 km/h (431 mph) was 11 km/h (6.8 mph) faster than that of the I-222. The I-224 was the last high-altitude fighter prototype developed by the MiG Design Bureau. (G.F. Petrov)

I-225

The I-225 was developed as a interceptor and not as a high-altitude fighter as were the I-220 to I-224 designs. The I-225 became the last MiG fighter to be developed during the Great Patriotic War. It received the MiG Design Bureau designation '5A.'

The I-225 was the rebuilt second I-220 prototype, but with a stronger structure and alloy components replacing most of the wooden parts of the I-220's wing. The armament of four ShVAK cannons was carried over from the second prototype of the I-220. In contrast to the I-220, no landing light was installed on the I-225.

The I-225 was equipped with an entirely new engine, the AM-42B, offering 2,000 hp at takeoff. At that time, the AM-42 was the most powerful engine available in the Soviet Union. The I-225 was equipped with an TK-300B turbosupercharger fitted on the starboard side, like its I-224 predecessor. The AM-42B drove an AV-5LV-22A propeller. The AM-42 engine had been developed by the Aleksandr Mikulin Design Bureau for the Il-10 assault aircraft, and in sharp contrast to the AM-39, which never left the development stage, the AM-42 was produced in large numbers. The AM-42B engine used in the I-225 was optimized for high altitude operation.

In contrast to the I-224, the I-225 was equipped with a considerably smaller intercooler under the front fuselage, mounted on the centerline.

The pilot sat in a pressurized cockpit manufactured of welded alloy. The windshield was armor glass of 64 mm (2.5 in) thickness, and a 9 mm (0.35 in) armor plate was installed behind the pilot's seat.

The I-225 prototype took off for its first flight on 21 July 1944 with Aleksey P. Yakimov at the controls. This was five months before the maiden flight of the I-224. On 7 August 1944, Yakimov reached a speed of 707 km/h (439 mph) at an altitude of 8,500 meters (27,887 ft), some 20 km/h (12 mph) less than the engineers had estimated. Rate of climb was 18.5 m/sec (3,645 ft/min).

The factory test program suffered a serious setback on 9 August 1944 when the landing gear retracting mechanism failed and the first I-225 prototype was damaged beyond economical repair in the landing. Fortunately, Yakimov survived the crash.

In order to continue with flight testing, a second prototype was built. This I-225 (serial number 02) was equipped with the more powerful AM-42FB engine delivering 2,200 hp at takeoff, two hundred more than the AM-42B. The AM-42FB received a new AMTK-1A turbosupercharger and an AV-5L-22B propeller.

The second I-225 prototype took off for its first flight on 14 March 1945. During its evaluation, it attained a remarkable 726 km/h (451 mph) at an altitude of 10,000 meters (32,808 ft). The second I-225 crashed during takeoff for its sixteenth flight on 26 April 1945, and the fuselage broke apart. Factory test trials were resumed in June 1945 after repair of the fuselage, but the trials were hampered by serious engine problems.

The I-225 was by far faster than other contemporary Lavochkin and Yakovlev fighter designs, with the exception of the Yak-3U. However, the problems with the AM-42 engine could not be fully solved, and development of the I-225 was discontinued in March 1947. It had become clear by then that future fighters would be jet-powered. (▶ 30)

▾ The second I-225 (serial number 02) was completed on 20 February 1945 and first flew on 14 March of the same year. The I-225 was powered by an AM-24FB engine rated at 2,200 hp at takeoff. It was painted overall gray with a long black panel on the starboard side. The national markings had a white border with a thin red outline. (Robert Bock)

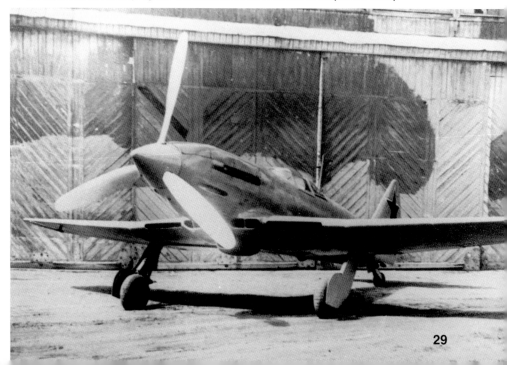

▾ The I-225 was the last conventional piston-engined fighter to be built by the MiG Design Bureau. It was also the sole MiG fighter to be powered by the AM-42 engine developed for the Il-10 assault aircraft. The second prototype I-225 crashed during takeoff on 26 April 1945, but was repaired. The I-225 program was terminated on 11 March 1947. (Robert Bock)

I-210 (MiG-9)

In May 1941, some five weeks before Nazi Germany attacked the Soviet Union, an order was issued by the *NKAP* to adopt the 1,676-horsepower M-82 radial engine for use on the MiG-3. The decision to use an alternative engine was a wise one. MiG-3 production had been interrupted in December 1941 due to the lack of AM-35A engines, but no loss in M-82 production was expected, because Molotov, in Siberia, was far out of range of the German Luftwaffe. Furthermore, with the M-82, which possessed 326 horsepower more than the AM-35A, the MiG Design Bureau also hoped to prolong the life of the MiG-3 design.

The M-82 fourteen-cylinder, two-row radial engine was developed by Arcadiy D. Shvetsov and his team in their Design Bureau at State Factory 19 at Molotov (since 1957, Perm) in central Russia. The M-82 had a seven-to-one compression ratio and used 94-octane fuel. With a two-speed supercharger, its nominal maximum continuous power was 1,540 hp at an altitude of 2,050 meters (6,725 ft).

The mating of the M-82, having a diameter of 1,260 mm (50 in), with the MiG-3's slimmer cross-section of 880 mm (35 in) was no simple task. It also was complicated by the differing thrust lines of the two engines and the substantially greater weight of the radial engine, which was 55 kg (121 lb) more than that of the AM-35A.

The new type received the MiG Design Bureau designation 'IKh' and the military designation 'I-210.' With the new engine, the fuselage of the I-210 was 172 mm (6¾ in) shorter than that of the MiG-3. The center of gravity was disturbed further by the elimination of the ventral radiator and the placement of an oil cooler under the nose. The fin area was slightly increased, and the I-210 received a rudder with an aerodynamic balance on top.

The I-210 was armed with three Berezin UBS 12.7 mm machine guns, one on either side of the engine, and the third on top of the nose on the aircraft centerline. Total ammunition supply for these three machine guns was 600 rounds.

The I-210 prototype (serial number 6501) first flew with Aleksey P. Yakimov at the controls on 23 July 1941, a month after the German attack against the Soviet Union. The prototype was followed by four pre-production I-210s that differed in some details from the first. On the spinner, a Hucks-type starter lug was added. Armament was augmented by a pair of ShKAS 7.62 mm machine guns placed above the Berezin UBS weapons. Each ShKAS had an ammunition supply of 650 rounds per gun. On the prototype, the barrels of the Berezin UBS were covered, but on the pre-production aircraft these covers were removed.

The I-210 had a top speed of 565 km/h (351 mph), 27 km/h (18 mph) less than that of the MiG-3. This was disappointing, as prior to the start of flight tests, the MiG Design Bureau had estimated a top speed of 630 km/h (391 mph).

Three pre-production I-210s (serial numbers 6503 to 6505) were sent for operational testing to the 34. *IAP* on the Kalinin front in June 1942. A fourth I-210 (serial number 6502) saw action with the 12th Guards Fighter Aviation Regiment. For these tests, the public designation 'MiG-9' was issued.

Performance and maneuverability of the I-210 were inferior to the MiG-3, and the I-210 was also plagued by strong vibrations that occurred in the tail. With all these shortcomings reported from the front, no more I-210s were built. The three I-210s assigned to the 34. *IAP* were returned to the MiG Design Bureau for modifications to their engines in late October. As soon as this work was completed, the I-210s were assigned to the 7. *Vozdushnaya Armiya* (7th Air Army) under the command of Colonel General F.P. Polynin on the Karelian front. These I-210s were not phased out until 1944, when the 7. *Vozdushnaya Armiya* retired from combat operation and was assigned to the reserve of *Stavka*.

▲ The I-210 was the first attempt of the MiG Design Bureau to mate the M-82A radial engine with the fuselage of the MiG-3. The cockpit canopy was enlarged on the I-210 and deepened to improve rear visibility. (G.F. Petrov)

▼ The first I-210. The M-82A engine had a takeoff rating of 1,676 hp and turned an AV-5L-156 propeller. (Sergei Kuznetsov)

I-211

The I-211 was an aerodynamically refined version of the I-210 powered by an ASh-82F engine, offering 1,850 hp, 174 hp more than the M-82. The significant increase in power was made possible by direct fuel injection, instead of conventional carburetors, but this output of 1,850 hp could only be maintained for ten minutes. The ASh-82F was developed by the Arcadiy D. Shvetsov Design Bureau at State Aircraft Factory 19 at Molotov.

There were a number of features introduced on the I-210 and I-211 that were considered real innovations within the *VVS*. On the order of the *NKAP*, all technical documentation on the engine cowling design, the proper positioning of the engine, and the wing leading edge slats were transferred to the Lavochkin Design Bureau in order to help improve the La-5 fighter. The MiG-developed slats also were introduced on the LaGG-3 (35 Series) fighter, helping to improve its poor handling qualities during landing.

The airframe of the I-211 was aerodynamically optimized based on the recommendations of *TsAGI*, which tested an I-210 in the T-101 wind tunnel at Kratovo. Most of the shortcomings of the I-210 were eliminated on the I-211. The cockpit section was moved 245 mm (9⅝ in) aft, and the vertical fin was enlarged, improving the fighter's directional stability. The I-210's oil cooler inlets on top of the engine cowling were replaced by wing root inlets, and the undernose oil cooler was deleted as well. The large single exhaust on the I-210 was replaced by two small exhaust stubs, and the large exhaust shield was deleted. The machine gun armament of the I-210 was replaced by two synchronized ShVAK 20 mm cannons located in the lower engine cowling. The windshield was swept back at a slightly greater angle, a sliding side window was added to the canopy, and the rear cockpit window was enlarged. The aerodynamic balance was removed from the rudder, and the wing slats were removed. The port pitot tube was relocated to the wing leading edge, and position lights were installed on top and bottom of each wing tip. The one-piece main wheel cover doors of the I-210 were replaced by two-piece doors on the I-211.

Only a single I-211 prototype was built. Assembly started in December 1942 in the MiG Design Bureau shops and was finished in late January 1943. The aircraft made its maiden flight on 24 February 1943 with Viktor Nikitovich Savkin at the controls. After having passed factory tests as well as State Acceptance Trials, the I-211 was assigned to the *NIIVVS*. Its pilots admired the I-211 highly because of its superb performance and handling qualities, which were considered to be superior to those of the contemporary La-5F and Yak-9. The I-211's top speed of 670 km/h (416 mph) was 22 km/h (14 mph) greater than that of the La-5FN, and the I-211 only needed four minutes to climb to an altitude of 5,000 meters (16,400 feet).

The I-211 was considered to be the best fighter in the inventory of the Soviet Air Force during the summer of 1943, and its mass production was recommended. However, there was no State Aircraft Factory available at the time to build the new MiG fighter in large quantities. Replacing the I-211 on the existing Lavochkin production lines in the four State Aircraft Factories was not possible, given that the work to convert the factories over to the new type would have consumed weeks or even months. At that stage of the war with Germany, fighters of any type were bitterly needed on the front. Accordingly, it was decided not to disrupt production of the Lavochkin fighters, and the I-211 was cancelled. (▸▸ 32)

I-210/I-211 Development

I-210

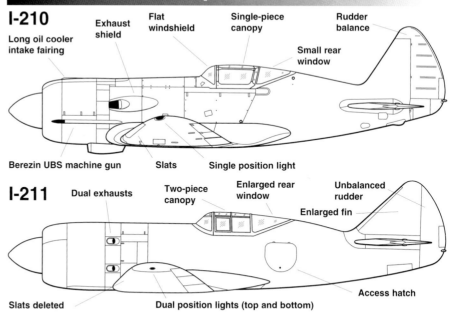

Long oil cooler intake fairing · Exhaust shield · Flat windshield · Single-piece canopy · Rudder balance · Small rear window · Berezin UBS machine gun · Slats · Single position light

I-211

Dual exhausts · Two-piece canopy · Enlarged rear window · Unbalanced rudder · Enlarged fin · Slats deleted · Dual position lights (top and bottom) · Access hatch

▸ The single I-211 prototype, which made its maiden flight on 24 February 1943. The I-211 was by far superior to the contemporary La-5FN, with a top speed of 670 km/h (416 mph), 22 km/h (13.7 mph) greater than that of the Lavochkin fighter. (Robert Bock)

DIS (MiG-5)

The twin-engined DIS (*Dvukhmotorny Istrebitel Soprovozhdeniya* — twin engined escort fighter) was developed primarily to escort the DB-3 and Pe-8 strategic bombers of the Soviet Air Force, and secondarily for long range reconnaissance, light bombing, or torpedo-dropping missions. As the Soviet Air Force showed interest in mass production of the DIS, the public designation 'MiG-5' was allocated.

Work on the DIS started in early 1940. The first twin-engine aircraft to be built by the MiG Design Bureau, it was powered by two AM-37 engines of 1,400 hp each. The fighter was equipped with two AV-5L-114 three-blade propellers. It was the first aircraft in the Soviet Union to have pneumatically operated landing gear.

The intended armament for the DIS was unusually heavy by Soviet standards: two Berezin UB 12.7 mm and four ShKAS 7.62 mm machine guns and a VYA 23 mm (.90-caliber) cannon in an under-fuselage pod. This formidable weapon was developed by A.A. Voronov and S.Y. Yartsev in 1940. Its shells could penetrate 25 mm (1 in) thick armor at a distance of 400 meters (1,312 ft). The cannon pod could be removed and a bomb load of 1,000 kilograms (2,205 lb) or a Type 45-36 torpedo carried instead.

The unarmed DIS prototype was built at State Aircraft Factory 1 at Moscow-Khodinka and took off for its maiden flight on 19 May 1941. State Acceptance Trials showed that the top speed of 560 km/h (348 mph) was some 104 km/h (65 mph) slower than calculated. In a measure to gain speed, two four-bladed AV-9B-L-149 propellers were installed, and some aerodynamic refinements were introduced. These increased top speed by 40 km/h (25 mph). The DIS prototype had a rate of climb of 15 m/sec (2,982 ft/min) to 5,000 meters (16,404 ft) and a range of 2,280 kilometers (1,417 miles).

▲ The **DIS** (*Dvukhmotorny Istrebitel Soprovozhdeniya* — twin-engined escort fighter) long-range escort fighter was powered by two AM-37 engines. The unarmed prototype first flew from Moscow-Khodinka on 19 May 1941. (Robert Bock)

▼ The second DIS-200 was powered by a pair of ASh-82 radial engines. Unlike the first, the main wheel cover doors were enlarged and bulged. The spinner was provided with Hucks-type starter lugs. The DIS-200 made its maiden flight on 22 January 1942. (Robert Bock)

DIS-200 (MiG-5)

It was originally intended to power the second DIS prototype with M-40 diesel engines offering 1,500 hp each. Diesels would theoretically provide the DIS with a longer range than gasoline powered engines, due to their low fuel consumption, but the M-40 had a number of problems that delayed its development. For this reason, the second DIS prototype was equipped with two ASh-82 fourteen-cylinder two-row radial engines of 1,676 hp each.

This second prototype received the MiG Design Bureau designation 'IT' and the military designation 'DIS-200.' The public designation 'MiG-5' was carried over from the first DIS.

Adoption of radial engines led to a redesign of the engine nacelles. In contrast to the DIS, the main wheel cover doors were enlarged and bulged. The DIS-200 was equipped with Hucks-type starter lugs on the propeller spinners.

Work on the DIS-200 started at Moscow-Khodinka, but when the State Aircraft Factory had to be evacuated, the unfinished DIS-200 was taken east to Kuibyshev. The DIS-200 took off for its maiden flight on 22 January 1942. The factory test program of the DIS-200 at Kazan came quickly to an end in 1942, when combat experience on the Eastern Front showed that there was no need for a long-range escort fighter. Most escort missions required for the Pe-2 and DB-3 bombers were of short duration and could be performed by the existing single-engine Lavochkin and Yakovlev fighters.

I-250 (N-1)

In early 1944 the State Committee for Defense gave an order to the MiG Design Bureau to develop a jet-powered fighter. Top priority was given to the project. The Kremlin had received intelligence that the Third Reich was test-flying a jet fighter, and in fact the first production examples of the Messerschmitt Me 262 jet fighter were just then coming off the assembly line at Leipheim in Bavaria.

The task of building a jet fighter proved to be difficult, as no functional jet engine was available in the Soviet Union at the time. The MiG Bureau therefore chose an unconventional power combination. The new fighter received a Klimov VK-107R that worked with a VRDK (*Vozdushno-Reaktivnyi Dvigatyel Kompressornyi* — air reaction engine compressor) jet boost system, a reaction unit intended to be used as an accelerator for a limited duration in crucial moments of air combat.

The VK-107R was a derivative of the VK-107A V-12 liquid-cooled engine rated at 1,650 hp at takeoff. The VK-107R drove a compressor which fed compressed air via a radiator through a duct to a mixing chamber in which fuel was introduced under pressure by a battery of seven injectors. The VRDK was operated by two levers on the pilot's port console. The compressor was driven by a drive shaft from the engine and could run at two speeds. Change of compressor speed was made automatically, excluding the possibility of pilot error. The combination Klimov VK-107R with the VRDK jet boost system received the designation E-30-20.

For takeoff and cruising, only the VK-107R was used, and the compressor ran at idle. When additional power was required, normal 95-octane aviation fuel was injected into the burners and ignited by the spark plugs. This power package offered a performance of 2,500 hp at 7,000 meters (22,966 ft). The VRDK supplied the majority of the power, a total of 1,350 hp. The maximum allowable running time for the VRDK was ten minutes. The VRDK could be engaged at all levels and flight modes, except during a climb.

The Soviet Air Force designation I-250 was allocated to the fighter, which received the MiG Design Bureau code 'N.'

The I-250 was the first reaction-powered MiG in history. It was a low-wing cantilever monoplane of all-metal construction. Initial armament included three ShVAK 20 mm cannons, which were replaced in the course of the evaluation by three lightweight B-20 20 mm cannons, each with an ammunition supply of one hundred rounds per weapon. One cannon was mounted between the cylinder banks, firing through the hollow reduction gearbox shaft and that of the propeller. The other two synchronized cannons were mounted side-by-side on the nose.

The first prototype, 'N-1,' was rolled out on 26 February 1945. Its maiden flight was delayed due to the absence of a flight-cleared E-30-20 power unit but finally occurred on 4 April 1945 with test pilot Aleksandr Pavlovich Dyeyev at the controls. The VK-107R and VRDK combination was tested for the first time on the third flight on 8 April 1945. During the tests a number of shortcomings were detected, including low compressor oil pressure and problems with the proper retraction of the main wheels. On 27 April 1945, the canopy disintegrated, and a second flight had to be terminated because of problems with the spark plugs.

On the other hand, the increase of power with the E-30-20 was impressive. During a test flight on 3 July 1945, the N-1 achieved a speed of 825 km/h (513 mph) at an altitude of 7,000 meters (22,966 ft). This was remarkably 170 km/h (106 mph) faster than the standard production La-7 fighter.

During the twenty-sixth flight of the first I-250 on 5 July 1945, its horizontal stabilizer disintegrated, and the plane crashed on final approach to Moscow-Khodinka airfield, killing test pilot Aleksandr Pavlovich Dyeyev. The crash investigation commission concluded that the cause was a high G-load, resulting from a sudden pitch-up at high speed and low level after up-elevator was applied.

(▸ 34)

▲ The I-250 (N-1) was powered by a conventional VK-107R engine and a VRDK auxiliary compressor. On a test flight on 3 July 1945, the N-1 achieved a remarkable speed of 825 km/h (513 mph) at an altitude of 7,000 meters (22,966 ft), 170 km/h (106 mph) faster than the standard production Lavochkin La-7 fighter. The first I-250 prototype was equipped with a retractable tailwheel. In the initial stage of flight tests, there was no auxiliary inlet below the exhaust stubs. (Robert Bock)

▼ In the course of the factory test evaluation, an auxiliary inlet was added below the exhaust stubs and the tail was slightly enlarged. During the 26th flight of the first I-250 on 5 July 1945, the horizontal stabilizer of the N-1 disintegrated, and the plane crashed on final approach to Moscow-Khodinka airfield, killing test pilot Aleksandr Pavlovich Dyeyev. (Robert Bock)

I-250 (N-2)

The second prototype of the I-250, called 'N-2,' became available in 19 May 1945 for the test program and made its maiden flight on 26 May 1945, reaching an altitude of 1,300 meters (4,265 ft). The second prototype differed in some details from the N-1. No armament was carried by the N-2, which also lacked a retractable tailwheel.

Like that of the N-1, the flight test program of the second prototype of the I-250 was not without incident. Recurring oil leaks in the compressor forced cancellation of several test flights, and the entire compressor unit was returned twice to the Central Aero-Engine Institute at Kratovo for repair. The installation of a new power unit was completed on 29 June 1945.

As a result of the fatal crash of the first prototype, the entire tail section of the N-2 was strengthened. The modified N-2 took off for the first time on 20 July 1945. During takeoff, test pilot Aleksey P. Yakimov reported excess torque to starboard and after landing advised Artyom I. Mikoyan that the aircraft not be flown again without modification. As a result of Yakimov's report, the vertical fin area was enlarged from 1.64 to 2.27 square meters (17.7 to 24.4 sq ft). The modified N-2 was flown on 14 August 1945, but with negative results, and as a result, a one-degree bias was subsequently applied to the fin.

Further test flights over the next several months revealed continued problems with oil leaks and excessive drag caused by the oil radiators. Three new oil radiators were delivered for the N-2 on 10 June 1946, but they did not fit inside the engine cowling. Modifications to solve this problem further delayed the test flights until 3 July 1946. On 12 July 1946, the N-2 performed its last flight. An engine fire resulted in a forced landing of the N-2 at Lyubertsy Aerodrome. The damage sustained in the landing, although substantial, was considered repairable, but with pre-production I-250 fighters available, the N-2 was no longer needed and was subsequently scrapped.

▲ The second prototype I-250 (N-2) differed from the first prototype in having an increased tail area and a non-retractable tailwheel. The N-2 also lacked any armament, while the N-1 was equipped with three B-20 cannons. Test pilot Aleksandr Pavlovich Dyeyev made the maiden flight of the N-2 on 26 May 1945. (Robert Bock)

▼ The second prototype was painted in gloss dark blue with a yellow-outlined red arrow. The N-2 suffered a forced landing at Lyubertsy Aerodrome on 12 July 1946 and was not repaired. (Robert Bock)

I-250 Development

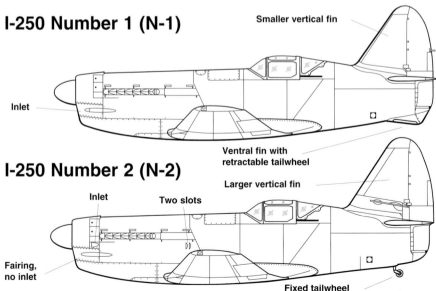

I-250 Number 1 (N-1)

Smaller vertical fin

Inlet

Ventral fin with retractable tailwheel

I-250 Number 2 (N-2)

Larger vertical fin

Inlet

Two slots

Fairing, no inlet

Fixed tailwheel

MiG-13

Although no State Acceptance Program was ever performed with the I-250, ten pre-production I-250s were ordered on 27 July 1945 by the *NKAP*, to be built at GAZ-381 (State Aircraft Factory 381) at Yaroslav. The schedule called for the delivery of the first two examples in September, followed by three in October and the remaining five aircraft during December 1945.

Production of the I-250 was plagued with difficulties from the beginning. The new aircraft type was a much more complex aircraft to build than the Lavochkin fighters previously built at GAZ-381, and completion of the aircraft was delayed by an inadequate number of qualified personnel and machine tools, a large number of design changes, a shortage of raw material, and delays in delivery of the E-30-20 power units. In late summer 1946 it was decided to deliver only eight I-250s to the *VVS*, and it was not until 30 October 1946 that these had been delivered.

These aircraft were allocated to pilots of the 176th Guards Fighter Aviation Regiment of the 324th Fighter Aviation Division, *PVO*. All were highly experienced in their Lavochkin La-7 fighters, but they disliked the I-250 completely due to its excessive high takeoff weight and limited power of the piston engine, ineffective rudder control during takeoff and landing, poor brakes, limited duration of the VRDK, the arrangement of the engine instruments, and a windshield which produced optical distortions.

An unsuccessful attempt was made to solicit interest in the I-250 from the *Aviatsiya Voyenno Morskogo Flota* (Soviet Naval Aviation). On 3 April 1948, the I-250 was officially withdrawn from the State Acceptance Program. This was some three months after the MiG-15 prototype took off for the first time, and it had become clear that the future lay with swept-wing jet-powered aircraft.

The public designation 'MiG-13' was assigned to the I-250, but was rarely used. (▶ 36)

MiG-13 Development

I-250 Number 2 (N-2)

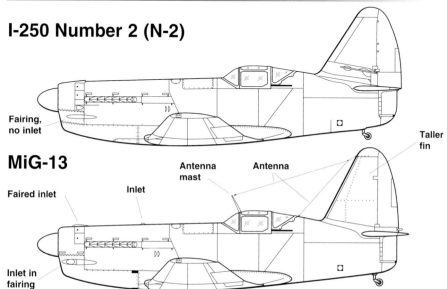

Fairing, no inlet

MiG-13

Faired inlet

Inlet

Antenna mast

Antenna

Taller fin

Inlet in fairing

▲ Removed cowling panels reveal the engine and accessories of the MiG-13. The production MiG-13 was powered by an VK-107R engine, a derivative of the VK-107A V-12 liquid-cooled engine rated at 1,650 hp at takeoff. (Robert Bock)

▼ Only ten MiG-13s were built, all at State Aircraft Factory 381 at Yaroslav. In contrast to the N-2, the MiG-13 had a taller tail and an antenna mast raked forward and to starboard. This is the second production MiG-13 (serial number 3810102), which was evaluated by the *Aviatsiya Voyenno Morskogo Flota* (Soviet Naval Aviation) at Skulte aerodrome near Riga on the Baltic Sea between 9 October 1947 and 3 April 1948. (Robert Bock)

I-270 (Zh-1)

The I-270 was a test bed for the RD-2M-3V dual-propellant rocket engine. Most of its fuselage characteristics were copied from the Messerschmitt Me 263V1 interceptor, which had been captured in an intact but unflyable condition in east Germany.

In February 1945, during the closing days of the Great Patriotic War, special commissions for captured equipment were formed and allocated to the Ukrainian as well as the Byelorussian front. Six war booty front-brigades with a total of thirty-four thousand specialists operated in east Germany, Czechoslovakia, Poland, and Hungary. The task of these units, under the command of Lieutenant-General Fyodor Vakhitov, was to capture examples of newly developed German weapons and send them immediately to the Soviet Union, where they could be closely examined. As many as 24,615 tanks, fifty thousand cars, and three million machine pistols were shipped from Germany to the Soviet Union.

A total of 213 German aircraft manufacturing facilities were discovered by Fyodor Vakhitov's specialists. Among the valuable prizes were three rocket-powered Messerschmitt Me 163B-0s, seven Me 163S trainers, and four intact Walter HWK 109-509A-2 rocket motors, as well as the full-scale wooden mock-up of the Me 263V1 captured at the Junkers plant at Dessau, Germany. The Me 263 was an improved variant of the Me 163B-0 with a retractable landing gear. The interceptor had been rolled out in March 1945, and a few towing tests were conducted the following month. It had been intended by the Germans to use an improved Walter HWK 109-509C-1 rocket motor in the Me 263, but it was never installed before the war ended.

The I-270 was based on the Messerschmitt Me 263V1, but instead of the swept wings used on the German interceptor, a conventional straight wing, having a leading edge sweep of twelve degrees, was chosen by the MiG Design Bureau for the I-270. The use of a conventional straight wing was due to a lack of experience with swept wings by the Central Aero and Hydrodynamics Institute at the time.

The fuselage of the I-270 was of circular semimonocoque construction. The cockpit was provided with a Heinkel Schleudersitzapparat ejection seat and was pressurized from air bottles. Armament consisted of two NS-23KM 23 mm cannons, which were located, together with the ammunition supply of forty rounds per gun, under the pilot's compartment.

The natural metal I-270 received a national insignia on the fin only. The red star had a large white border narrowly outlined in red. A red design was painted on the underside of the nose.

As the intended RD-2M-3V rocket motor was not available on time, the first I-270 (Zh-1) made its maiden flight as a glider in late December 1946. After being towed by a twin-engined Tupolev Tu-2 bomber to the required altitude, the Zh-1 was released and glided back to earth. The trials quickly revealed that landing a powerless Zh-1 was far from easy.

The practice of towing powerless rocket fighters was not new in the Soviet Union. During 1945 and 1946, several such flights were conducted with captured Messerschmitt Me 163B-0s and Me 163Ss, both towed to altitude by a Tu-2. During these trials, at least one Me 163B-0 was lost. One of the main tasks of the test program was to establish whether rocket aircraft could be safely landed without engine power. The data gained during these tests were also passed to the engineers and pilots performing the Zh-1 test program.

The engineless factory test trials of the I-270 were of short duration and ended abruptly in early 1947. A few weeks after its maiden flight, the Zh-1 was written off during a belly landing. The MiG Design Bureau test pilot Viktor N. Yuganov survived the crash to become on 30 December 1947 the first pilot to fly the S-01, the prototype for the MiG-15. (▸ 38)

▼ The first prototype of the I-270/Zh-1 lacked an engine and was towed by a twin-engined Tupolev Tu-2 bomber. Its flight program started in late 1946 and continued to early 1947, when it was written off in a crash landing. The lower nose as well the stripes were painted in red. (Robert Bock)

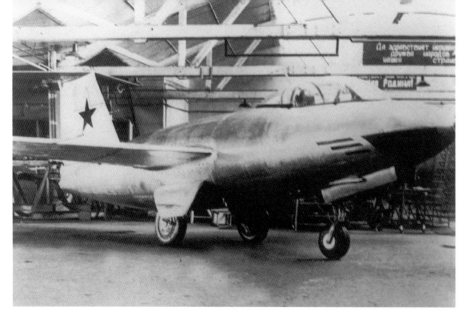

The brand-new Zh-1 shortly after its completion in the shops of the MiG Design Bureau in late 1946. Many features of its fuselage construction were adopted from the Messerschmitt Me 263V1 prototype, which had been captured by the Soviets in the Eastern part of the Third Reich. However, in contrast to the German interceptor, the I-270 was had straight wings. (Robert Bock)

The Zh-1 had a very narrow main wheel track of only 1.6 meters (5 ft 3 in). A towing attachment was mounted on its nose. (Robert Bock)

The Zh-1 started its flight test program in late 1946, but as the RD-2M-3V rocket engine was not available, the tests were conducted without an engine. The fuselage design of the Zh-1 was very similar to the Messerschmitt Me 263V1, but the I-270's horizontal stabilizer was fitted atop the tail. On the Zh-1, the U-shaped elevator hinges were not covered. (Robert Bock)

I-270 (Zh-2)

In contrast to the unpowered Zh-1, the second I-270 (Zh-2) was equipped with an RD-2M-3V rocket engine. The RD-2M-3V was developed by Valentin P. Glushko and Leonid S. Dushkin at Experimental Design Bureau 16. The rocket engine had a maximum thrust of 1,449 kg (3,195 pounds) and was fueled by a mixture of nitric acid, kerosene, and hydrogen peroxide. All propellants were stored in three sets of tanks: 1,620 kilograms (3,571 lb) of nitric acid in four tanks, 440 kilograms (970 lb) of kerosene in one tank, and 60 kilograms (132 lb) of hydrogen peroxide in seven tanks.

The propellant turbopumps were driven by two generators, one powered by the aircraft's electrical system, and a second, powered by the windmilling action of a small impeller in the nose, that served as a backup. The impeller had been taken from a Messerschmitt Me 163B-0 that had been shipped to the Soviet Union.

The Zh-2 differed in some minor details from the Zh-1, including bulged nose gear doors, shorter cannon fairings, covered elevator hinges, and the addition of an EKSR-46 flare dispenser on the port lower fuselage and a vent on the underside.

The Zh-2 became available in early January 1947 and was flown for the first time with the RD-2M-3V engine by Viktor N. Yuganov. The Zh-2 reached a speed of 936 km/h (582 mph) at 15,000 meters (49,213 ft). Its service ceiling was 17,000 meters (55,774 ft) and it took 2.37 minutes to climb to 10,000 meters (32,808 ft).

The Zh-2 was destroyed in an landing accident in spring 1947. The evaluation trials showed that the I-270 was very impractical and unsuited for service operation. The rocket engine was dangerous and allowed a powered flight duration of only nine minutes.

▲ The Zh-2 differed in a number of details from the Zh-1. The towing attachment on the nose was replaced by an impeller taken from a captured Messerschmitt Me 163B-0. A blister was added to the upper nose, and the nose wheel doors were bulged. An EKSR-46 flare dispenser was added to the lower port rear fuselage. (Robert Bock)

▼ The Zh-2 was equipped with an RD-2M-3V rocket engine of only nine minutes duration. The RD-2M-3V had been developed by Valentin P. Glushko and Leonid S. Dushkin at Experimental Design Bureau 16. National markings were applied to the rear fuselage and tail as well as to the lower wing surfaces. (Robert Bock)

I-270 Development

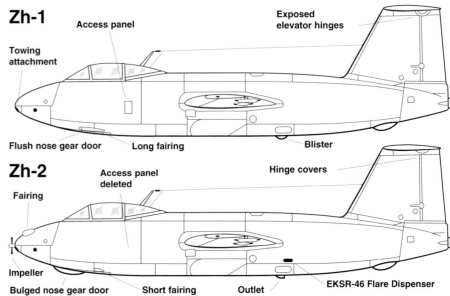

Zh-1
- Access panel
- Exposed elevator hinges
- Towing attachment
- Flush nose gear door
- Long fairing
- Blister

Zh-2
- Access panel deleted
- Hinge covers
- Fairing
- Impeller
- Bulged nose gear door
- Short fairing
- Outlet
- EKSR-46 Flare Dispenser

I-300 (MiG-9)

The MiG-9 was in many aspects an epoch-making aircraft. Not only was it the first jet fighter developed by the MiG Design Bureau, it was also the first pure jet-powered fighter in the Soviet Union. It served as an interim solution until the more advanced MiG-15 'Fagot' became available.

The origin of the jet engine goes back to 1909, when the Frenchman Jean Delouvier presented the first theoretical studies of a reaction motor. At the 1910 International Air Show at Paris, Romanian engineer Henri Coanda unveiled the first aircraft to be powered by a turbine. In 1930, British officer Frank Whittle patented his idea of a jet engine using a centrifugal compressor and a combustion chamber. In Germany, the Heinkel works at Rostock developed the first practical jet engine in the world, the He-S2, conceived by physicist Dr. Hans-Joachim Pabst von Ohain. An improved version, the He-S3B, powered the He-178V1 experimental aircraft, which performed the world's first flight of a jet powered aircraft on 27th August 1936 with Flugkapitän (pilot) Erich Warsitz at the controls. On 15 May 1941 the first British jet, the Gloster E.28/39 took off for its maiden flight, powered by a Whittle engine. The first American jet, the Bell XP-59A flew for the first time on 31 September 1942.

However, it was the Third Reich that had the world's first operational jet fighter, Messerschmitt's Me 262, the first prototype of which made its maiden flight on 25 March 1942. The first intelligence reports on the Me 262 were in Allied hands by January 1943, and top priority was given in London and Washington to the development of jet fighters that could be mass produced. England's Gloster Meteor flew for the first time on 5 March 1943, and the prototype of the American Lockheed P-80A Shooting Star took off for its maiden flight on 8 January 1944.

The Soviet Union, however, lagged behind the technical capabilities of its Western Allies. Even more alarming, the Soviets had knowledge in spring 1944 that Germany would not only produce the jet-powered Me 262A-1, but also the Arado Ar 234 jet bomber. It became clear that the German jet aircraft would easily outclass the conventional Soviet piston-engined fighters. Accordingly, on 22 May 1944 the State Committee for Defense issued an order to the Yakovlev, Sukhoi, and MiG Design Bureaus to start development of jet-engined fighters. The MiG Design Bureau allocated the designation 'F' to its project. Its Soviet Air Force designation was 'I-300.'

At that time, no reliable Soviet jet engine existed, and this situation did not change until the end of the war. The Soviet Union for a long time had failed to appreciate the advantages of the jet over piston engines, and research on and development of jet engines had been modest, at best. In 1940, Arkhip M. Lyulka had developed the Soviet's first experimental jet engine, having a thrust of 714 kg (1,574 lb). However, the German attack on the Soviet Union in summer 1941 gave a new impetus to jet engine development, and in 1943, Lyulka and his design team began the development of the S-18 jet engine with a thrust of 1,275 kg (2,810 lb) . Its derivative, the TR-1, with a thrust of 1,326 kg (2,923 lb), was tested in early 1945.

During its advances into Eastern Germany, Czechoslovakia, and Poland, the Red Army had captured a number of German jet engines, and a total of twenty Jumo 004B-2 and fifteen BMW 003A-1 were shipped to the Soviet Union. A number of these were allocated to the All Union Institute for Aviation Materials and the Central Aero-Engine Institute, and an initial investigation by Soviet engineers concluded that the German engine designs were much more promising for further development than the TR-1 engine. Accordingly, on 5 August 1945, Aleksey Hachuring, the People's Commissar of the Aviation Industry, issued an order to the MiG Design Bureau to built a twin-engined fighter that could accommodate the BMW 003A-1 engines. With the same order, the State Factory 16 at Kazan was entrusted in building the BMW 003A-1. To fulfill this task, the former Bavarian Motor Works plant at Basdorf-Zühlsdorf near Berlin, which had produced

▲ The MiG-9 was the great-grandmother of all jet-powered MiG fighters, and the prototype MiG-9/I-300 (F-1) was the first Soviet jet to fly. This historic event took place 24 April 1946, when Aleksey Nikolayevich Grinchik took off from Kratovo (Ramenskoye) with the F-1 prototype. The I-300 was powered by two German BMW 003A-1 engines that had been built in the Bavarian Motor Works plant at Basdorf-Zühlsdorf. (G.F. Petrov)

the BMW 003A-1, was dismantled, and the entire factory, complete with all its tools and equipment, was transported to State Factory 16 on the Volga river. In addition, eight former Bavarian Motor Works specialists were assigned to State Factory 16. A total of three captured BMW 003A-1 engines were supplied to the MiG Design Bureau. Two of these German engines were intended to power the new Soviet jet.

Work on the first I-300 prototype started in summer 1945. Fast, jet-powered fighters with exceptionally heavy cannon armament were regarded by the Soviet supreme command as the most effective weapons against the new threat posed by American atomic bombers. The requirement issued by the Soviet Air Force called for a fighter with a top speed of 900 km/h (559 mph) and an armament of a single Nudelman N-57 57 mm (2.24-caliber) and two Nudelman-Suranov NS-23KM 23 mm (.90-caliber) cannons. The N-57 weighed 135 kg (298 lb) and had a rate of fire of 230 rounds per minute and a muzzle velocity of 600 meters (1,920 feet) per second.

With a requirement for such heavy armament, the initial design of the I-300 called for the installation of the engines in the wings in order to leave room in the fuselage for the cannons, in a configuration reminiscent of the Messerschmitt Me 262. However, preliminary wind tunnel tests conducted at *TsAGI* indicated that with this configuration it would be impossible to attain the required speed.

The design of the heavily-armed fighter was seriously constrained by the limitations of the Soviet aviation industry and the stringent requirement of the Soviet supreme command to have a turbojet-equipped interceptor in its inventory at shortest notice. In order to comply, the MiG Design Bureau radically revised the original project. Data on swept wings was lacking, so the designers chose a conventional, straight-wing configuration. As the turbojet engine was lighter than a piston engine, the armament and cockpit were moved forward in order to (▸▸ 40) maintain the center of gravity, a change which also improved the pilot's field of vision to forward and below. The engines now were to be grouped in the forward fuselage section, in an arrangement which wind tunnel tests had indicated was aerodynamically more efficient. On the other hand, this redesign required measures to protect the fuselage underside from the hot jet exhaust and to solve problems related to uneven airflow over the tail caused by the exhaust.

On 6 March 1946, the fully armed fighter was completed. The F-1 performed its first ground taxiing tests at Kratovo. Taxiing trials revealed a tendency for the nose of the I-300 to pitch up when thrust was applied. The fuselage tail section was redesigned and rebuilt, and no more pitch-up occurred on the ground.

Another problem was discovered in the fuselage surfaces adjacent to the nozzles of the BMW 003A-1 engines. Heat-resistant steel plating had been attached to the skin of the airframe to protect it from the jet exhaust. However, the plating and the dural skin were expanding at different rates, causing deformation of the fuselage surface. To overcome this problem, the steel plate was replaced by a screen equipped with an air cooling system.

In mid-April 1946, the F-1 was ready for its flight tests. On 12 April 1946, the first high-speed trials were performed at Kratovo. A week later, on 19 April, the aircraft made a hop to an altitude of 4 meters (13 ft). On 24 April 1946, at 1112 hours, the F-1 made history by becoming the first Soviet jet to take to the air. Test pilot Aleksey Nikolayevich Grinchik performed two circuits over Kratovo and landed six minutes later. Almost ten years after the first flight of a jet-powered aircraft in Nazi Germany, the Soviet Union had finally entered the jet age with MiG's I-300.

Flight testing of the F-1 continued for the next three months, and maximum recorded ceiling and speed increased with each succeeding flight. During one of the test flights, a speed of Mach 0.78 was recorded, exceeding the 900 km/h (559 mph) demanded by the Soviet Air Force. During the test program, severe buffeting was encountered around or behind the engine, but this was cured by introducing steel-sandwich heat shields downstream of the jet nozzles.

The test program continued successfully until 11 July 1946, when, at a demonstration of the I-300 for the top echelons of the Ministry of Aviation Production, test pilot Aleksey N. Grinchik, who had already performed nineteen successful evaluation flights in the F-1, was killed in the crash of the prototype before the assembled crowd of dignitaries. The accident investigation established that the crash was a result of an in-flight aileron structural failure during high speed at low level. Until its crash, the F-1 had flown a total of just six hours and twenty-three minutes.

As no other prototype was ready, the flight test program had to be suspended until early August 1946, when two additional I-300 prototypes, the F-2 and F-3, became available. These also were powered by a pair of original German BMW 003A-1 engines. The F-2 prototype was taken to the Central Aero and Hydrodynamics Institute for wind tunnel testing, which explored the effects of jet exhaust upon flight stability, thermal aspects of its construction, and vibration of the tail.

The I-300 received the public designation 'MiG-9,' and the type was introduced to the public during the Tushino Air Display on 18 August 1946, alongside the Yak-15 turbojet fighter.

In November 1946, the flight test program ended, and the I-300 was recommended for series production and service within the Soviet Air Force.

▼ **Test pilot Aleksey Nikolayevich Grinchik (second from right) talks with the ground crew in front of the first I-300 prototype. In contrast to the production MiG-9, this plane was equipped with an N-57 cannon housing in the intake duct. Grinchik was killed in this particular I-300 on its twentieth test flight during a demonstration for the top echelons of the Ministry of Aviation Production on 11 July 1946. (G.F. Petrov)**

I-301 (MiG-9)

Reflecting the urgency with which the Soviet Air Force wished to press the MiG-9 into operational service, the *MAP* (*Ministerstvo Aviatsionnoi Promyshlennostil* — Ministry for Aircraft Production) ordered a pre-production batch of ten MiG-9s on 28 August 1946, three months before flight tests of the I-300 prototype were completed. The MiG Design Bureau allocated the designation 'FS' to the series-built MiG-9, which received the Soviet military designation 'I-301.' The ten MiG-9s were produced at GAZ-1 at Kuybishev (now Samara) on the Volga river. During World War II, this plant had produced a large number of Ilyushin Il-2 assault aircraft.

The first pre-production MiG-9 (serial number 106001) left the assembly line on 13 October 1946, the last (serial number 106010) on 22 October 1946. These first ten pre-production examples of the MiG-9 were powered by captured Bavarian Motor Works BMW 003A-1 engines, which received the Soviet designation RD-20A-1. Most of these had been found during the closing days of World War II by the advancing Red Army at Basdorf-Zühlsdorf near Berlin. During World War II, the Bavarian Motor Works manufactured about seven hundred engines of this type.

Copying the BMW 003A-1 engine was not without its troubles, even though the former Bavarian Motor Works plant at Basdorf-Zühlsdorf had been dismantled and all production facilities, including 868 machine tools, transported to State Factory 16 at Kazan on the Volga river. The original schedule called for thirty RD-20A-2 engines, as the Soviet-built copies were to be known, to be available in late 1945, but the deadline passed without any RD-20A-2s having been produced. Neither the original German equipment nor the know-how of German specialists could prevent State Factory 16 from encountering serious problems.

There were two factors responsible for the delay. While the Soviet Union had captured all the hardware to produce the BMW 003A-1 engine, all the technical documentation and drawings had been captured by the US Army at Strassfurt, Saxony, in April 1945. In addition, the Soviet metal industry encountered difficulties in producing heat resistant alloys, necessary for trouble-free operation of the RD-20A-2. As a result, the engine life was restricted to only fifty hours, a shorter life than that of the original German BMW 003A-1 engine.

The MiG-9s were built at Kuibyshev and were shipped in crates by rail to Kratovo, where they were re-assembled and test flown. The first MiG-9 arrived on 5 October 1946, and in less than a month, all ten pre-production I-301s had been assembled and flown. Apart from their armament, the pre-production MiG-9s were identical to the prototype I-300. These MiG-9s were demonstrated to the public for the first time during a ceremonial flypast over Moscow on 7th November 1946.

On the pre-production MiG-9s the heavy and unsuitable 57 mm N-57 cannon of the F-1 prototype was replaced by the brand new Nudelman N-37 37 mm (1.46 in) cannon. Armament also included two Nudelman Suranov NS-23KM 23 mm (.90 in) cannons placed in the lower nose. Total ammunition supply was 160 23 mm shells and forty 37 mm shells.

In autumn 1946, the pre-production MiG-9s were allocated to the Scientific Research Institute of the Soviet Air Force for its State Acceptance evaluation program. During these test flights the horizontal stabilizer failed on two occasions, necessitating immediate structural modifications. A larger vertical fin with a dorsal fillet improved directional stability. The rudder trim tab was deleted. The Elektron magnesium alloy skin of the elevator and rudder was replaced by duralumin, and the rudder structure was strengthened. The engine exhaust nozzles became smaller and more conical. The lower fuselage access panel was enlarged in order to make access to the cannons easier. The two conical inlets on each side under the wing became rectangular. Inboard portions of the ailerons were modified in such a way that they could be used as a speed brake. An additional lead-in (▶ 43)

▲ The production MiG-9 (I-301) received a ventral fin that was absent from the I-300 prototype, and the cannon barrels of the two NS-23KM cannons were shortened. The production MiG-9 carried a N-37 cannon in the air intake duct. (Sergei Kuznetsov)

MiG-9 Development

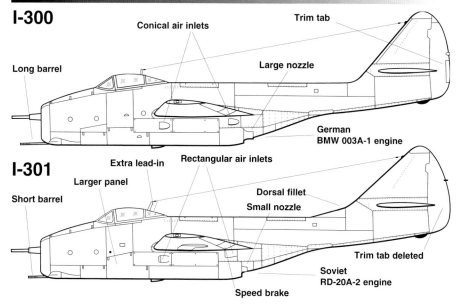

I-300

Long barrel — Conical air inlets — Trim tab — Large nozzle — German BMW 003A-1 engine

I-301

Short barrel — Larger panel — Extra lead-in — Rectangular air inlets — Dorsal fillet — Small nozzle — Trim tab deleted — Soviet RD-20A-2 engine — Speed brake

MiG-9 Specifications

Length . . . . 9.83 m (32 ft 3 in)
Wingspan . . . . 10 m (32 ft 9¾ in)
Height . . . . 3.225 m (10 ft 7 in)
Weight, empty . . . 3,420 kg (7,540 lb)
Weight, maximum . 4,963 kg (10,941 lb)
Engine . . . . One RD-20A-2 (BMW 003A) turbojet
of 800 kg (1,764 lb) thrust
Maximum speed . . 910 km/hr (565 mph)
Range . . . . 800 km (497 mi)
Rate of climb . . . . 19.4 m/sec (3,731 ft/min)
Service ceiling . . . 13,500 m (44,291 ft)
Armament . . . . One N-37 37 mm (1.46-in) cannon
Two NS-23KM 23 mm (.90-in) cannons

cable was added from the large antenna cable into the starboard fuselage. The long NS-23KM cannon barrels of the prototype were replaced by short cannon barrels. New and more effective brakes were installed on the main wheels.

The pre-production I-301 had a top speed of 911 km/h (566 mph) at an altitude of 5,000 meters (16,404 ft), a considerable improvement over piston engined fighters. However, the climb rate of the MiG-9 was only slightly superior to that of the Lavochkin La-7 radial-engined fighter. Takeoff performance of the MiG-9 was sluggish, compared to piston-engined fighters, whose propellers provided far greater thrust at takeoff speeds than did the RD-20A-2 turbojets. The takeoff run of the MiG-9 was 950 meters (3,117 ft), compared to the 345 meters (1,132 ft) of the Yakovlev Yak-3.

In July 1948 the first MiG-9s were issued to operational Fighter Aviation Regiments of the 1st Air Army. A total of 604 MiG-9s of all variants was produced until late 1948, when the I-301 was replaced by the MiG-15 'Fagot-A' on the production line of GAZ-1. The US Air Force originally gave the MiG-9 the designation 'Type 1,' subsequently replacing it with NATO's Air Standardization Coordinating Committee reporting name 'Fargo.'

The MiG-9 was a cantilever mid-wing monoplane of all-metal construction. The semimonocoque fuselage was flush-riveted. The air intake structure included the nosewheel and the gun bay. The streamlined cabin glazing comprised a fixed windshield with a jettisonable canopy. Pilot armor consisted of two 12 mm (0.5 in) steel plates and a 55 mm (2.16 in) armor glass windshield. The pilot seat was of dural construction, attached to the cabin floor by a set of brackets. The cockpit was unpressurized. Instrumentation was spartan.

The wing was of two-spar construction, attached to the fuselage at the roots. Flight controls were by mechanical linkage to elevator and ailerons, and by cables to the rudder. The port elevator trimmer was electrically operated.

The MiG-9 did not reach critical Mach numbers, so did not require many aerodynamic refinements. Its general aerodynamic configuration differed little from that of piston-engined fighters. The MiG-9 became an ideal trainer upon which a considerable proportion of Soviet pilots learned skills which proved to be highly valuable when the time came to convert to the transonic MiG-15 fighters.

Chinese MiG-9s

The People's Republic of China became the sole export customer for the MiG-9. On 14 February 1950, the People's Republic and the Soviet Union entered into a "Treaty of Friendship, Alliance, and Mutual Assistance," and in accordance with the treaty, a vast number of Soviet aircraft were delivered to China, including 250 MiG-9s. These aircraft were all former *VVS* fighters that became obsolete after the introduction of the MiG-15 'Fagot,' but Chinese MiG-9s became operational four weeks after the introduction of the MiG-15 in the *Chung-kuo Shen Min Tai-Fang-Tsun Pu-Tai* (Air Force of the People's Liberation Army).

Chinese pilots were instructed by Soviet personnel. The first MiG-9s were assigned in November 1950 to the 16 *Quzhu Tuan* (16th Fighter Aviation Regiment) and the 17 *Quzhu Tuan* (17th Fighter Aviation Regiment), of the *Kong 6 Shi* (6th Aviation Division). Both units were based at Anshan Air Force Base in the province of Liaoning. Four more MiG-9 units became operational during December 1950. The 19 *Quzhu Tuan* (19th Fighter Aviation Regiment) and the 21 *Quzhu Tuan* (21st Fighter Aviation Regiment) belonged to the *Kong 7 Shi* (7th Aviation Division) and were based at Dongfeng Xian in the province of Jilin. The 34 *Quzhu Tuan* (34th Fighter Aviation Regiment) and the 36 *Quzhu Tuan* (36th Fighter Aviation Regiment) were part of the *Kong 12 Shi* (12th Aviation Division) and were based at Xiaoshan Xian in the province of Zhejiang. Many Chinese pilots who first flew in a MiG-9 subsequently saw action over Korea in the cockpit of a MiG-15.   (▸▸ 44)

▲ Production MiG-9s were equipped with speed brakes, which could open up to ninety degrees, in the ailerons. The prototypes lacked speed brakes. On the MiG-9 the trim tab on the rudder was deleted. (Sergei Kuznetsov)

▾ A production MiG-9 during evaluation with the Scientific Research Institute of the Soviet Air Force. The number '22' on the fin was red with a thin white outline. (Sergei Kuznetsov)

Armament Development

I-301 (MiG-9)

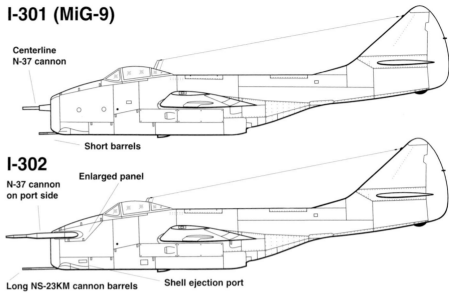

Centerline
N-37 cannon

Short barrels

I-302

N-37 cannon
on port side

Enlarged panel

Long NS-23KM cannon barrels

Shell ejection port

▲ The I-302 was developed to overcome the problem of engine flameout which occurred when all three cannon were firing. Trials were performed in the winter of 1947, but the tests revealed that this cannon arrangement could not prevent flameout. (Robert Bock)

▼ On the I-302, the N-37 cannon barrel was lengthened and moved to the port side of the nose. The upper access panel had to be enlarged, and a shell ejection port was cut in the lower nose. The two NS-23KM cannon barrels were also lengthened. (Robert Bock)

I-302

The I-302 was an attempt to overcome the problem of MiG-9 engine flameout caused by ingestion of gun gases when all three of the aircraft's cannons were fired at once. This aircraft received the MiG Design Bureau Designation 'FP.'

A standard production MiG-9 was converted as a testbed. The centerline Nudelman N-37 cannon was moved to the port side, the barrel lengthened, and the cannon covered by a fairing. The port access panel on top of the nose was enlarged and a shell ejection port for the N-37's cartridges was added to the port side of the nose. The two NS-23KM cannon barrels were also significantly lengthened.

The MiG Design Bureau expected that with this armament configuration, the flameout would be eliminated, as the cannon blast was produced farther ahead of the air intake. A number of test firings were performed with the I-302 in early 1947. These failed to solve the problem, but also revealed that the firing of the NS-23KM cannons mounted low in the nose was not to blame. Since the tests did not produce the expected results, the project was phased out. There was just a single I-302 built. Most of the test program was carried out by Viktor Nikolayevich Yuganov, who on 30 December 1947 would make the maiden flight of the MiG-15 prototype.

The I-302 was painted light grey overall with the lower portion of the rear fuselage painted black. National insignia, in the form of red stars with large white border and a thin red outline, were applied on the rear fuselage and the rudder as well as to the wing undersurfaces.

I-305 Development

I-301

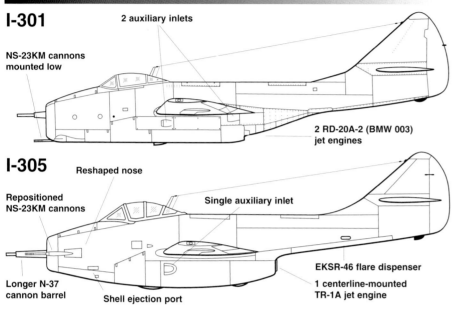

NS-23KM cannons mounted low

2 auxiliary inlets

2 RD-20A-2 (BMW 003) jet engines

I-305

Reshaped nose

Repositioned NS-23KM cannons

Single auxiliary inlet

Longer N-37 cannon barrel

Shell ejection port

EKSR-46 flare dispenser

1 centerline-mounted TR-1A jet engine

I-305

The I-305 was a derivative of the I-301 equipped with a single TR-1A engine, completed by the MiG Bureau at Zhukovsky (previously known as Kratovo) in November 1947 and developed as a backup in case of failure of the MiG-15, the first prototype of which was then nearing completion. The TR-1A was an entirely Soviet design developed under the leadership of Arkhip M. Lyulka.

The first prototype TR-1 engine was tested in early 1945, but it suffered from problems that never were solved completely. The TR-1A was a more powerful derivative of the TR-1, with an output of 1,500 kg (3,307 lb) thrust, only 100 kg (220 lb) less than both RD-20As in the I-301 combined. The use of a single engine reduced the I-305's empty weight by 350 kilograms (772 lb).

The rear fuselage had to be redesigned in order to accommodate the TR-1A, and the extreme aft fuselage was narrowed to accommodate future installation of an afterburner. The entire nose section was redesigned and became more conical as a result. The two NS-23KM cannons were repositioned to the middle of the nose, level with the N-37 cannon. Shell ejection ports were located on both sides of the nose. The barrels of all three cannons were lengthened.

The I-305 was equipped with a pressurized cabin, and below the cockpit, an inlet for the cockpit pressurization air was added on both sides. An ejection seat was also fitted.

The I-305 was almost complete in November 1947, when news was received that the TR-1A turbojet had suffered failures in testing and was not yet ready for operation. Shortly thereafter, on 30 December 1947, the MiG-15 prototype took off on its maiden flight. The MiG-15's swept wing was considered by far superior to the I-305's straight wing, and with the TR-1A engine not ready, the I-305 was scrapped without ever having flown. (▸ 46)

▲ The I-305 was almost completed in late 1947, when the project was cancelled in favor of the MiG-15. It was intended to power the I-305 with a single TR-1A engine of 1,500 kg (3,307 lb) thrust. (Robert Bock)

▼ The I-305 was armed with two NS-23KM cannons and a single N-37 cannon installed at the same level. The starboard NS-23KM had a blister aft of it. The nose of the I-305 had a more tapered, conical shape than that of the MiG-9. (Robert Bock)

▲ The I-307 *Babochkoi* ('Butterfly') was fitted with a large hollow vane on the cover of the N-37 cannon barrel, which was also lengthened. The shape resembled a butterfly, hence the name. Hot gases from the cannon's muzzle were sucked into a slot in the vane's leading edge and then vented away from the nose intake through slots at the top and bottom of the vane. (Robert Bock)

Nose Variation

MiG-9

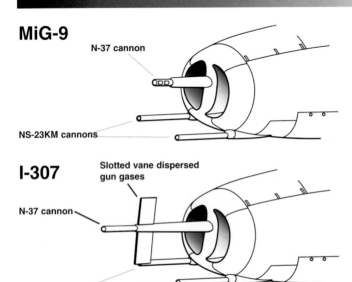

I-307

I-307 (MiG-9)

The I-307 was an improved version of the MiG-9, powered by a pair of RD-20F engines. The RD-20F, which was subsequently redesignated RD-21, was an improved version of the RD-20A-2, developed at State Factory 16 at Kazan and built from components exclusively manufactured in the Soviet Union. The RD-21 afforded an increase in thrust of 200 kg (441 lb) to 1,000 kg (2,205 lb), which was achieved by increasing the fuel flow and raising the turbine temperature and speed.

Equipped with the new engine, the I-307 reached a top speed of 950 km/h (590 mph), 40 km/h (25 mph) faster than the standard production MiG-9. The brakes were also improved, in response to various complaints from Soviet pilots about insufficient brake power during landing.

The first I-307 flew in September 1947 with Ivan T. Ivashchkenko, who three years later would make the first flight of the MiG-17 prototype, at the controls. A small series of I-307s was built. Externally, the I-307 could not be distinguished from the I-301.

I-307 'Babochkoi'

The I-307 'Babochkoi' (butterfly) was another attempt to overcome the problem of flameout of both engines when all cannons were fired, a serious and dangerous problem that reduced the combat readiness of the MiG-9. This problem had been encountered for the first time during the State Acceptance Trials of the I-301 in late 1946. Test pilot Andrey G. Kochetkov was test firing the N-37 cannon at an altitude of 7,500 meters (24,606 ft), when the two RD-20A-2 engines flamed out after the first shells were fired.

Initially, the MiG engineers assumed that the flameout of the engines was a problem specific to the MiG-9. However, this was a problem that occurred on most first-generation jet aircraft and one which took years to resolve. It was ultimately discovered that gases from the explosion of the cannon shells' propulsive charge were entering the engines and producing a compressor surge, causing the engines to flame out.

A series of trials with the MiG-9 was performed in an attempt to overcome the problem, but it was never fully solved during the operational service of the jet fighter. The flameout occurred only when all three cannons were firing, but not when firing just the two NS-23KM cannon mounted low in the nose.

The 'Babochkoi' was fitted with a large hollow vane mounted vertically on the fairing of the N-37 cannon barrel, which was also lengthened. The hot gases from the cannon's muzzle were sucked into a slot in the plate's leading edge and then vented out through other slots at the top and the bottom of the plate, deflecting them away from the engine intake. The MiG engineers hoped this would eliminate the flameout of the RD-21 engines.

The shape of the device resembled a butterfly, hence the name for the modified I-307. The first tests, carried out in late 1948, revealed that the problem of flameout was not solved by the 'butterfly' device, which only increased the MiG-9s drag and reduced its directional stability, making aiming in combat difficult. As it had become clear that the MiG-9 in due course would be replaced by the more advanced MiG-15, there were no further tests carried out to overcome the MiG-9's flameout problem. Due to a different arrangement of its weapons, the MiG-15 did not suffer from flameout caused by ingestion of gun gases.

I-308 (MiG-9M)

The I-308 was an extensively revised variant of the I-301 fighter, developed as a back-up in case the swept-wing MiG-15 proved to be a failure. It was the last member of the MiG-9 family to be developed from the I-300.

The I-308 prototype was completed at the MiG Bureau Design Shop at Zhukovsky in June 1947, six months before the MiG-15 prototype was ready for flight testing, and first flew in July 1947 with Viktor N. Yuganov at the controls. The factory flight tests of the I-308 were completed in April 1948.

The MiG-9M was equipped with a pair of RD-21 engines, and with a top speed of 965 km/h (600 mph) was the fastest fighter of the entire MiG-9 family. It was also the sole MiG-9 to exceed a speed of Mach 0.8. With the new, more powerful engines, ceiling and rate of climb improved as well. The MiG-9M could climb to an altitude of 5,000 meters (16,404 ft) in 2.7 minutes, compared to 4.3 minutes for the I-301.

The nose of the I-308 was completely redesigned, and the cockpit relocated forward. The cockpit also was pressurized and an ejection seat fitted. The cannons were installed with their muzzles behind the air intake in an attempt to solve the flameout problem plaguing the MiG-9.

State Acceptance Trials of the I-308 started in spring 1948 and ended that September. Test pilots were not pleased. One of the shortcomings of the I-308 was the flameout of the engines under certain flight conditions during gun trials at altitudes above 8,000 meters (26,246 feet). However, it was the spectacular new swept-wing MiG-15 that proved to be the death knell for the MiG-9M as well as other first-generation, straight-wing jet fighters such as the Yakovlev Yak-23. In view of the promising results of the MiG-15 trials, the Soviet Air Force rejected the MiG-9M, and its further development was stopped by the MiG Design Bureau. (▸▸ 48)

MiG-9M Development

MiG-9

N-37 cannon

Two auxiliary inlets

Two RD-20A-2 jet engines of 1,764 lb thrust each

NS-23KM cannon mounted low

MiG-9M

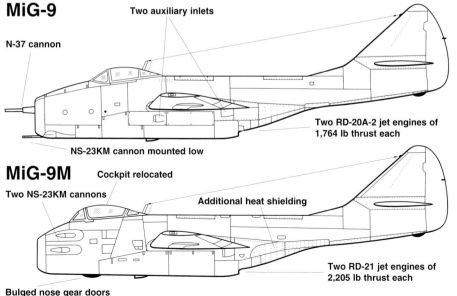

Two NS-23KM cannons

Cockpit relocated

Additional heat shielding

Two RD-21 jet engines of 2,205 lb thrust each

Bulged nose gear doors

▲ The MiG-9M became the last derivative of the MiG-9 family and its fastest variant. Additional heat shields were fitted on the aft fuselage due to the increased combustion temperatures of the RD-21 engine. (Robert Bock)

▾ The entire nose section of the MiG-9M was modified, and the two NS-23KM cannons were relocated to the port side. The N-37 cannon was placed on the starboard side of the nose, level with the NS-23KM cannons. This arrangement was chosen in an attempt to overcome the flameout phenomenon that had plagued earlier variants. The main wheel cover doors were bulged on the lower leading edge. (Robert Bock)

I-301T (MiG-9UTI)

Both the Soviet Air Force and the MiG Design Bureau recognized the need for a trainer version of the Soviet Union's first turbojet-powered fighter, and work on such a two-seat version began in May 1946, a month after the maiden flight of the I-300 prototype. The trainer received the MiG Design Bureau designation 'FT' and the Soviet military designation I-301T. In October 1946, the first mockup of the trainer was unveiled, and two prototypes, designated 'FT-1' and 'FT-2,' were ordered. Its public designation 'MiG-9UTI' was not issued until January 1948.

The prototype FT-1, completed in December 1946, was a converted MiG-9 fighter from the first production batch, powered by two German BWM 003A-1 engines. A second, slightly raised cockpit for the instructor, fitted with the same instrumentation as the front cockpit, was installed in place of a fuselage fuel tank. The FT-1 received ejection seats which were Soviet copies of the Heinkel ejection seat used on the Heinkel He 162A-2. Armament of the FT-1 was the same as the MiG-9 fighter, but with a reduced ammunition supply. Empty weight of the FT-1 was 3,349 kilograms (7,383 lb), 184 kilograms (406 lb) more than the MiG-9 fighter.

The FT-1 was first flown in early April 1947. Test pilots were not pleased with the MiG-9 trainer. The main shortcoming was limited vision for the instructor during takeoff and landing, the most critical moments of a training flight with an inexperienced pupil. In spite of this, the MiG-9UTI was recommended for serial production. However, when it became clear that the MiG-9 would be soon replaced by the swept wing MiG-15, all orders for the trainer version of the MiG-9 were cancelled. Only the two MiG-9UTI prototypes, FT-1 and FT-2, were built.

The FT-2 served as a testbed for further trials of the Soviet copy of the Heinkel Schleudersitzapparat ejection seat, the most advanced ejection seat in the world at the end of World War II. The seat was improved for use in the MiG-9 and subsequently for the MiG-15.

▲ The first prototype of the MiG-9UTI trainer (FT-1) was completed in December 1946 and rolled out on 17 January 1947. The FT-1 was powered by two German BMW 003A-1 engines. Overall dimensions remained the same as those of the fighter variant. To make room for the rear instructor's cockpit, a fuselage fuel tank had to be deleted and a second tank reduced in size. (Robert Bock)

▼ The FT-2 prototype first flew on 15 July 1947 was equipped with a 235-liter (62-gallon) drop tank on each wing tip. An SPU-2M intercom system enabled communication between pupil (front) and instructor (rear). The front canopy opened to starboard, while the rear canopy slid aft to open. (Sergei Kuznetsov)

MiG-9UTI Development

MiG-9

Single aft-sliding canopy

Short cannon barrel

MiG-9UTI

Additional window

Rear aft-sliding canopy

Forward starboard-opening canopy

Long cannon barrel

EKSR-46 flare dispenser

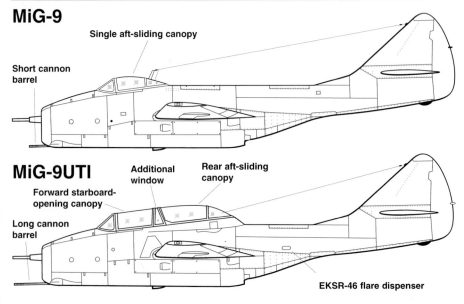

MiG-9L

In late 1947, the MiG Design Bureau began development of the KS-1 *Komet* (Comet — NATO designation AS-1 'Kennel') anti-ship cruise missile. The KS-1 was initially carried by the Tu-4K 'Bull,' but its main launch platform from 1955 onwards was the Tu-16KS 'Badger B.' After launch, the KS-1 proceeded, guided by an AP-23 autopilot, toward its target. As soon as the K-1M *Kompleks* nose radar detected the target, guidance was switched to automatic homing. The KS-1 was powered by a RD-500 centrifugal-flow turbojet (a Soviet copy of the Rolls-Royce Derwent V engine) with a thrust of 1,590 kg (3,505 lb), and had a range of 150 kilometers (93 miles) at a cruising speed of 800 km/h (497 mph). The KS-1 served in Soviet Naval Aviation between 1953 and 1966. Some KS-1s were exported to Indonesia, and a shore-based version was supplied to the Soviet Navy as well as to China, Cuba, Egypt, and Poland.

In parallel with the development of the KS-1, its radar and guidance systems were flight-tested aboard a heavily converted MiG-9 fighter, designated 'MiG-9L.' Its MiG Design Bureau designation was 'FK,' the second letter standing for '*Komet*.' Trials began in 1949 with a Tu-4KS serving as a parent aircraft.

Compared to the I-301, the fuselage was lengthened by 0.37 meter (1 ft 2½ in) to 10.12 meters (33 ft 2½ in), while the wingspan remained unchanged. The armament was removed. On top of the air intake, the K-1M *Kompleks* radar was installed inside a radome. A tube-shaped receiver antenna was installed on the leading edge of each wing. These antennas picked up the reflected emissions from the *Kompleks* radar.

The MiG-9 L had a crew of two. An unpressurized compartment for the systems operator with a bubble canopy was placed in the rear fuselage, replacing the fuselage tanks of the fighter. A pod on top of the tail housed the *Kobalt-N* transmitter and receiver antennas.

MiG-9L Development

MiG-9UTI

Cannon armament

MiG-9L

Kompleks radar in nose radome

Second cockpit for system operator

Kobalt-N transmitter and receiver

Armament deleted

Receiver antenna

▼ The MiG-9L served as a testbed for the guidance system of the KS-1 *Komet* (Comet) anti-ship cruise missile (NATO designation AS-1 'Kennel'). The *Kompleks* radar was installed in a radome above the air intake, and receiver antennas were installed in tube-shaped fairings on the wing leading edge. A pod housing antennas for the *Kobalt-N* transmitter and receiver was fitted to the top of the vertical fin. A second cockpit for the system operator was placed in the rear fuselage. (Robert Bock)